Differentiated Assessment Strategies

We dedicate this book to teachers, staff developers, and administrators who Zap the Gaps in their students' learning journeys.

Differentiated Assessment Strategies

One Tool Doesn't Fit All

Carolyn Chapman • Rita King

Foreword by **Marti Richardson**

CORWIN PRESS, INC.
A Sage Publications Company
Thousand Oaks, California

For information:

 Corwin Press
A Sage Publications Company
2455 Teller Road
Thousand Oaks, California 91320
www.corwinpress.com

Sage Publications Ltd.
1 Oliver's Yard
55 City Road
London EC1Y 1SP
United Kingdom

Sage Publications India Pvt. Ltd.
B-42, Panchsheel Enclave
Post Box 4109
New Delhi 110 017 India

Printed in the United States of America

Library of Congress Cataloging-in-Publication Data

Chapman, Carolyn, 1945-
Differentiated assessment strategies: One tool doesn't fit all /
Carolyn Chapman, Rita King.
        p. cm.
Includes bibliographical references and index.
    ISBN 0-7619-8891-2 (cloth) — ISBN 0-7619-8890-4 (pbk.)
1. Educational tests and measurements. 2. Individualized instruction.
3. Mixed ability grouping in education. I. King, Rita G. II. Title.
LB3051.C4483 2005
371.26—dc22   2004018751

This book is printed on acid-free paper.

    06   07   08   09   10   9   8   7   6   5   4

Acquisitions Editor:	Jean Ward
Production Editor:	Diane S. Foster
Copy Editor:	Mark Newton, Publications Services
Typesetter:	C&M Digitals (P) Ltd.
Proofreader:	Scott Oney
Indexer:	Gloria Tierney
Cover Designer:	Tracy E. Miller
Graphic Designer:	Lisa Miller

Contents

Research is opening horizons to new understanding of how students learn. Exploring how students remember and what it means leads teachers to use intriguing strategies that capture and maintain engagement in activities and assignments. This chapter explains the compelling rationale for using a wide variety of differentiated assessment tools before, during, and after learning.

A physical environment that is efficient, engaging, safe, and nurturing is essential for instruction and assessment. This chapter shows teachers how to establish an effective classroom climate for a community of learners in which each person feels that he or she is a valued, contributing member. Teachers will find tools here for assessing and addressing the learning climate to meet students' cognitive and affective needs and optimize success. This chapter is designed to promote emotional intelligence, self-efficacy, motivation, behaviors for self-regulated learning, and celebrations of success.

Acknowledgments

A special thank-you to Jim Chapman for his constant support, encouragement, and patience. His guidance and advice, as always, kept us on track.

A special thank-you to Jean Ward, our editor, for her support, expertise, and suggestions. Deep appreciation is extended to Douglas Rife, Faye Zucker, Anita Linton, and everyone on the Corwin Press staff for their assistance. Thank you to Arcie Luna, Ce Ce Sisneros, and Amelia Iribarren for their "after-hours" support for all of our endeavors.

Our appreciation is extended to Marti Richardson, who honored us by writing the foreword. Liz Bennett, another special friend and admired educator, shared her expertise and encouraged us. Brad O'Gwynne and Amy Blanton assisted with their expert knowledge of technology.

We thank the teachers who participated in our training sessions. They used the strategies and gave us valuable, constructive feedback. Our gratitude is extended to professional developers and administrators who continue to support us because they believe our strategies, programs, and philosophies make a difference for today's students.

About the Authors

Carolyn Chapman continues her life's goal as an international educational consultant, author, and teacher. She supports educators in their process of change for today's students. She has taught in kindergarten and college classrooms. Her interactive, hands-on, professional development opportunities focus on challenging the mind to ensure success for learners of all ages. She walks her walk and talks her talk to make a difference in the journey of learning in today's classrooms.

She authored *If the Shoe Fits . . . How to Develop Multiple Intelligences in the Classroom and Sail Into Differentiated Instruction*. She coauthored *Multiple Assessments for Multiple Intelligences, Multiple Intelligences Through Centers and Projects, Differentiated Instructional Strategies for Reading in the Content Areas, Differentiated Instructional Strategies for Writing in the Content Areas, Differentiated Instructional Strategies: One Size Doesn't Fit All,* and *Test Success in the Brain-Compatible Classroom*. Video Journal of Education, Inc., features her in *Differentiated Instruction*. Her company, Creative Learning Connection, Inc., has also produced a CD, *Carolyn Chapman's Making the Shoe Fit*. Each of these publications demonstrates her desire and determination to make an effective impact for educators and students. She may be contacted through the Creative Learning Connection Web site at www .carolynchapman.com or at cchapman@csranet.com.

 **Rita King** is an international consultant, trainer, and keynote speaker. She conducts sessions for teachers, administrators, and parents on local, state, and international levels. Her areas of expertise include differentiated learning, assessment, multiple intelligences, practical applications of brain-based research, reading and writing strategies, creating effective learning environments, and strategies for test success.

She is an adjunct professor in the Department of Educational Leadership at Middle Tennessee State University. She has more than 20 years of teacher-training experience. As principal and director of the university's teacher-training program in the laboratory school, she has taught methods courses and conducted demonstration lessons. Her doctorate degree is in Educational Leadership. Her formal training (EdD, EdS, MA, and BS) has been directly related to education and teacher training.

She coauthored *Differentiated Instructional Strategies for Reading in the Content Areas, Differentiated Instructional Strategies for Writing in the Content Areas,* and *Test Success in the Brain-Compatible Classroom.*

Her sessions give educators and parents innovative, engaging activities to develop students as self-directed, independent learners. Participants enjoy her practical, easy-to-use strategies; sense of humor; enthusiasm; and genuine desire to foster the love of learning. She may be reached via e-mail at kingrs@bellsouth.net.

Foreword

Differentiated Assessment:
One Size Doesn't Fit All

At the age of six, I determined that prizes in "goody" boxes were desirable treasures for me. I looked forward to taking my meager allowance with me on my weekly jaunt to the grocery store with my mother to buy myself a treat. Often it was a box of Cracker Jack popcorn. After receiving the box from a clerk behind the counter, the first thing I would do was dig for the prize that was buried deep within the special corn. How exciting it was to find the little ring, compass, or tiny car! I loved it at that moment and played with it for a while, but the toy soon found its way to a wastebasket because it was made with flimsy material and broke easily or it got lost in the bottom of my toy box.

Two generations later, I find that my three grandchildren like to go to McDonald's to get a Happy Meal. It didn't take me long to determine why! The first trip revealed the answer. The Happy Meal comes with a prize! Do children eat their food first and then open the prize? No! The first thing they do is move the drink off the tray onto the table, place the hamburger on one side of the tray, french fries on the other, and pick up the prize to unwrap. This prize lasts as a favorite toy for a few hours, and then it, too, follows the same path that my prize in the Cracker Jack popcorn followed years ago.

None of these toys that seem wonderful at first glance have the capacity to wow children for any significant length of time. They are not treasures that will endure. In fact, they are inane. They lack substance. To have value and substance, the object should have worth that will be highly regarded and will have sustained power over time. The Cracker Jack prizes and the gifts in the Happy Meal don't pass the test of time, substance, or worth.

Adults are more critical than children about trinkets that they receive. Through years of experience in giving and receiving, most adults have learned to be discriminating about something that is offered as a prize or a reward. They note the distinctive features and immediately know if they have been given something that will be useful or long-lasting. The decision they make about the item usually determines whether it will be hidden away in the closet, placed at the back of a drawer, put out on the desk, or placed on a shelf for easy viewing or reference.

The book that you are holding in your hand, *Differentiated Assessment Strategies: One Tool Doesn't Fit All*, is an adult-level gem that will have abiding value for educators. It is a bible for assessment strategies that you will keep nearby for easy reference in planning and implementing classroom assessment. It will be useful for all teachers, principals, and supervisors who construct development plans with teachers, staff, curriculum developers, and program designers. The material has been authoritatively integrated with the latest research on the topic of assessment with a plethora of ideas and makes grounded connections between assessment principles and well-planned activities. The use of this book will take the mystery out of how to guide and monitor students' performances over time in multiple situations. This is important as schools focus on continuous growth for all through both individual and school improvement!

The authors of this "prize," Carolyn Chapman and Rita King, have experience in producing quality educational resources. They have worked on the growth edge of research in each of their previous books and have given educators topic-specific implementation strategies to use that bridge the gap between knowing and doing. Now Chapman and King build on their previous service and present a book on differentiated assessment. They have notched up their work a bit by presenting assessment strategies that are high-energy and results oriented. Their labor will transform the way you gather information about students' achievement and inspire you to engage in new ways of thinking, learning, and instructing. Champions in their efforts, they have created a "present" just for you and present it to you now as a unique resource that you will use over and over again.

Assessment was chosen as the topic for this book because of its importance. It is so important that it may be said that it is a cardinal element of a restructured education system. It is *the* linchpin for school improvement! In 1998, Michael Fullan said, "assessment has to drive the educational change agenda around learning and student achievement." That has come to pass. Many noted scholars have set about the task of doing the research that is necessary to help the novice understand this agenda. As they learn more about assessment and evaluation, each of the researchers addresses the profound changes that are taking place in standards, instruction, learning goals, evaluation techniques, and even teacher preparation. They speak to the need for us to make assessment part of instruction rather than separate from it, and emphasize that it must be an ongoing and integral part of the learning process.

Rick Stiggins, a highly respected member of the assessment and evaluation community, wrote that we must see assessment with *new eyes* in a June 2002 article in the *Phi Delta Kappan* titled "Assessment Crisis: The Absence of Assessment FOR Learning." He went on to say, however, that few teachers are prepared to make critical decisions about instructional assessment. Veteran teachers confuse assessment with evaluation and may use their information for grading purposes only. New teachers are coming to the classroom ill-prepared to know how to gather evidence to monitor students' progress, provide meaningful and immediate feedback to students on what they need to do to achieve thoughtful outcomes, and then revise their instruction to achieve the desired ends. Staff development programs are helping some teachers with the topic, but they are a lucky few that have access to quality learning. The vast majority of educators, which Stiggins refers to as our national faculty, are trying to revise their instructional techniques to incorporate assessment *for* learning in a meaningful way with little assistance. The worst scenario is that many teachers still don't know that they need assistance.

Chapman and King understand the staff development needs of teachers and the challenges from research. They have used that comprehension and their new eyes to provide all educators with a major resource of enduring value for their instructional assessment tool kit. To use the authors' words, they have effectively "zapped the gap" between knowing and doing by using the book to give you, the reader, direct instruction on how to implement assessment that is well planned, formatted, and designed to acknowledge the fact that students have multiple abilities, talents, and skills that cause them to learn in many different ways.

The focus of the book honors 10 research-based assessment principles that support individual achievement and offers a differentiated assessment system that you may use to plan effectively; focus on how students learn and make it central to your classroom practice; enhance your professional skill; be sensitive and constructive; foster motivation; promote understanding of goals and criteria; help learners know how to improve; develop the capacity for self-assessment; and recognize educational achievement (principles adapted from the commissioned work of Black and Wiliam, 2002) by the *Assessment Reform Group*, www.assessment-reform-group.org.uk). Chapman and King give us a unique illustrative model of all 10 principles.

Throughout the book there is a clear and constant focus, which is related to the six goals that are stated early in the book. I would use one phrase to synthesize the goal-oriented approach: "Chapman and King have placed value on the individual." They continually speak to the fact that individual students need differentiation because the methods of assessment must align with each new instructional goal and measure whether or not it has been achieved. Differentiation may also be noted as important because educators need all the tools at their disposal to assess student knowledge. The book does this and encourages you to build on the growth edge of each student. The authors then give you a map to help you achieve that end.

Of particular interest to me is the challenge presented by the authors to each of us to provide opportunities for *all* students to use higher-order thinking skills. That supports a figurative soapbox of mine from which I preach that every child can learn the next thing that follows the last thing that he or she learned. We now know enough about how the brain works and which instructional strategies to use to learn specific tasks to make this happen. With differentiated assessment, task analyses, and goal-focused instruction, even low-achievers can learn to high standards and succeed with higher-order thinking skills.

The assessment agenda for this country has been set. The researchers have acknowledged it and established the rationale for urgency. The challenge before us is great! Because assessment must be an integral part of instruction, more resources like *Differentiated Assessment Strategies: One Tool Doesn't Fit All* are needed to help us learn the art and science of effectively implementing the process. A greater need, however, is for you and me, and all our colleagues, to make a commitment to use a "classroom assessment process and the continuous flow of information about student achievement that it provides in order to advance student learning" (Stiggins, 2001). We can do this collectively if we each make a decision to do the following:

1. Start early. We must take a proactive approach to changing the way we treat assessment in the classroom. If we are proactive, we will focus on preparing. Therefore, it is imperative that we educate ourselves now about the process. Options may include joining a study group, reading books and educational journals, studying student data, and having assessment conversations with colleagues. Standards should be reviewed and then used as a starting point for assessing the understanding of students. Appropriate instruction can then be planned.

2. Start small. The bigger the change required in instructional style, the more intimidating it will be for us. My suggestion, therefore, is to start using differentiated assessment in a small way. Let's focus on a few, specific tools that will allow us to see the growth of students through *new eyes*. We can increase the range and variety of strategies we use as we learn and grow ourselves.

3. Start now. The first reason for us to focus on assessing in a differentiated mode is that we will be more deliberate in our instruction. Student learning will be the "prize" for which we search, and we will find it through the process of assessment. The value of our prize will increase

as we continually use varying strategies to provide valid and sufficient evidence that students have achieved appropriate learning goals. The second reason to start now is the most important: students deserve the best we have to offer!

All of this may require us to change. John Maxwell, a best-selling author, says that there are three kinds of people when it comes to change:

- Those who don't know what to do
- Those who know what to do but don't do it
- Those who know what to do and follow through

This book will help the third kind of person because the reader will learn what to do. The concepts that are presented are sound, and the strategies that are described are practical to implement and thorough; therefore, the third person will have everything needed to implement an action plan. Will you be like the third person? Is it worth the effort for your children? You can be revolutionary and effect change that will be sustaining by incorporating assessment into your daily instruction and differentiating it to serve multiple styles of learning. The future of each student you teach, or reach, depends on it. You will serve your learners well by rethinking and refining your instructional strategies, allowing room in your present structure for some innovation, and offering classroom activities that are flexible to your students' needs. When you make a decision to do this you will be deliberately giving a gift to your students that will have quality and value. You really can do no less.

Marti Richardson
Past President, National Staff
Development Council

Introduction

One Tool Doesn't Fit All

Effective teachers strategically select an appropriate assessment tool for each learning situation. In the same way that a carpenter chooses a hammer to drive a nail and a saw to cut a board, the teacher chooses the right tool for each purpose. Rich data is gathered using a wide variety of instruments. This allows students to show what they know in more than one way. In short, it takes more than one form of assessment, or more than one tool, to gauge individual learning.

WHAT IS DIFFERENTIATED ASSESSMENT?

Differentiated assessment is an ongoing process through which teachers gather data before, during, and after instruction from multiple sources to identify learners' needs and strengths. Students are differentiated in their knowledge and skills. They differ in the ways and speeds at which they process new learning and connect it to prior knowledge and understanding. They also differ in the ways they most effectively demonstrate their progress.

Choosing the Right Tools

The carpenter uses his expertise to choose the right tool for the procedure, the materials, and the task at hand. The same principles apply to teachers and students on a far more sophisticated and consequential level. The teacher who plans instruction to accommodate the differences among students designs or selects the best preassessment tools. This reveals students' unique knowledge, prior experiences, abilities, learning styles, multiple intelligences, motivations, behaviors, interests, and attitudes. The results are used to strategically customize instructional plans, provide students with multiple ways to show their learning, keep them on the right track, and accelerate their learning journeys.

Ongoing Assessment

Formal testing emphasizes assessment *of* learning. It is an evaluation of the student's progress at the end of a unit or a period of time. Compare it to a final building inspection. Before calling for the final inspection, the builder conducts ongoing progress checks at all stages of construction. Think about the value of ongoing assessment *for* learning, or informal assessment.

For another perspective on the importance of ongoing assessments for learning, picture the following scene. A race car has arrived on the track for a major race. Before the race begins, the crew and driver thoroughly check their car's engine, tires, brakes, and safety equipment. During the race, they continue to assess the vehicle so it maintains maximum performance and speed. The driver occasionally pulls into the pit so the crew can replace parts, add fuel, change tires, and provide other needed services. If the driver and crew wait until the end of the race to monitor the car's performance, it will be too late to make repairs and adjustments. Think about a learner's performance in the classroom. Is it reasonable to wait until the end of a unit, a semester, or a set period of time to assess his or her performance?

Clarifying the Differentiated Assessment Terminology

The following definitions are presented to clarify the ways the terms are used in this resource:

Assessment: a judgment or appraisal of the learner's work and specific needs. The direction for immediate and future instruction is based on information gathered with formal or informal procedures

Assessment Activity: an exercise that actively engages the student, physically or cognitively, in the assessment process

Assessment Choices: ways to provide the learner with assessment options, such as a report or a demonstration. Providing choices is a powerful change that immediately differentiates and empowers learners

Assessment Skill: the learner's effectiveness and proficiency in applying an assessment tool. For example, the ability to use a matrix to record information is a skill in using a graphic organizer strategy

Assessment Strategy: a plan or procedure used to reach a goal. Journaling can be used as an assessment strategy during learning or as a way to develop a cumulative record of learning. Remember, a strategy is the umbrella for skills and tools. It is more global.

Assessment Tool: a way to assess the student. The assessment tools include activities or devices that provide information or data for instructional planning before, during, and after learning. For example, a reflective sentence starter such as "I don't understand" is a tool for metacognition

Authentic Assessment: an analysis of the learner's skills, abilities, and strengths through a variety of observable indicators. This includes skill performances, purposeful activities, portfolios, demonstrations, hands-on experiences, and projects

Evaluation: a summative analysis of the learner's abilities and skills at a particular time to make judgments. Evaluation data is traditionally gathered at the end of a unit of study, a semester, or the year

Formal Assessment: tools that collect specific, observable information. This data may be derived from content knowledge, skills and abilities, or behavior observations. Tests, pop quizzes, checklists, rubrics, and Likert scales are examples of formal assessment tools

Formative Assessment: ongoing assessment before, during, and after instruction to identify needs and provide continuous feedback so the student learns more effectively. Usually only selected results from identified formative assessments are averaged and included in a formal grade

Informal Assessment: tools that gather information from spontaneous, gut reactions for the moment. Response cards and hand signals that indicate individual knowledge of a topic or skill are examples of informal assessments

Ipsative Assessment: describes a form of metacognitive self-assessment by which the learner compares a present performance with a prior performance to measure improvement and address needs

Standard: a benchmark or level of mastery for specific skills. These objectives are usually established by the state or district for each grade level and subject area

Summative Assessment: assessments that occur at the end of a period of instruction to measure achievement. The results are usually used as evidence for a grade, for reporting to parents, to identify award recipients, or to make placement decisions

ANALYZING YOUR VIEW OF DIFFERENTIATED ASSESSMENT

Consider the following questions as a preassessment of your disposition toward differentiated assessment, related teaching experiences, and beliefs in relation to this philosophy.

In your teaching, do you do the following:

- Use assessment results to identify a student's needs
- Use informal and formal assessment data to plan instruction
- Plan to meet the unique strengths and needs of the student
- Believe a student's interest and attitude related to a specific topic directly impacts his or her academic success

If you answered "yes" to some or all of these questions, you are aware of the need for differentiated assessment strategies. "Differentiation is a philosophy that enables teachers to plan strategically in order to reach the needs of the diverse learners in classrooms today" (Gregory & Chapman, 2001, p. x). Differentiated assessment identifies a learner's needs and strengths. The teacher uses a variety of formal and informal assessment tools to reveal the student's knowledge base, prior experiences, interest level, attitude, and ability in relation to a topic or skill. The results guide the teacher's strategic plans to meet individual needs.

The Goals of This Book

Our goals in writing this resource include the following:

- To give teachers differentiated assessment tools, strategies, and activities to identify a student's strengths and needs
- To provide teachers with assessment strategies they can give students to empower them as self-directed learners
- To apply the latest research related to effective assessment techniques
- To present novel assessment tools that provide immediate feedback for teachers and learners
- To provide teachers and learners a variety of assessment tools that are easy to remember and apply
- To emphasize the value of creating a positive learning culture for assessment experiences

Building the Toolbox to "Zap the Gaps"

Differentiated instruction and assessment go hand in hand. Marzano (2000) clarifies the goals of assessment and instruction as follows:

- Assessment should focus on students' use of knowledge and complex reasoning rather than their recall of low-level information.
- Instruction must reflect the best of what we know about how learning occurs.

To support this high level of instruction and assessment, the teacher needs a constant stream of assessment data. The authors present differentiated assessment strategies and an overflowing box of tools to assess students before, during, and after learning. These tools are designed to help teachers identify students' needs or holes in learning when they appear, so students can "zap the gaps" and expedite learning.

Differentiation has been pondered, questioned, and researched since teachers first considered the best way to reach individual students. Today as research and technology provide more details about how the brain learns and how assessment supports, we predict that differentiated instruction and differentiated assessment will become common practices. Practical applications of the research are found in the various strategies and activities presented throughout this book. More research is embedded in the methods, models, and approaches to differentiated assessment.

We hope educators use these differentiated assessment tools to personalize assessment experiences. We have designed or selected numerous strategies, activities, and ideas so teachers can strategically adapt them to guide students in their personal learning journeys.

WILL DIFFERENTIATED ASSESSMENT BRING ALL STUDENTS ALONG AND LEAVE NO CHILD BEHIND?

Federal guidelines now emphasize the value of embedding assessment in instruction and using the information to guide planning. To accomplish this task, the teacher selects or designs the best assessment tools and activities to gather individual data before, during, and after the learning. The information is analyzed, and the results are used to tailor lesson plans for students.

Differentiated assessment is a prerequisite to curriculum planning and instruction. Formative assessment activities and strategies provide data from which to make teaching decisions for differentiation to address the many ways students vary in their experiences and knowledge base. Consider the three-group scenario presented in the following metaphor: Imagine that you are viewing a class assessment through a magnifying glass. A close look at the results reveals that one group needs the background information expanded for them to provide a stronger foundation related to the topic. The second group possesses the knowledge and background needed to begin the lesson. The third group is ready to accelerate beyond the basics, to expand their knowledge and explore or investigate new areas related to the topic.

(Text continues on page xxvi)

We offer the following acronym as a reminder to all of us of how to strategically apply differentiated assessment strategies.

Analyze individual strengths and needs

Strategically plan for each learner to improve and excel

Set new objectives

Explore abilities

Supply assistance and appropriate materials

Stress growth

Monitor for immediate intervention

Empower with self-directed assessment strategies

Nurture and support efforts

Translate needs and strengths into active learning

Post this list on your wall and in your heart. Share it with your students, their parents, and your learning community to help students become lifelong metacognitive learners.

Figure 0.1 Overview of Tools and Strategies for Differentiated Assessment

Brain Research	Creating the Climate	Knowing the Learner	Assessment Before and During	Assessment After Instruction	Differentiated Learning Models and Tools
Information Processing and Memory Personal Connections Transfer Novelty Automaticity **Develop Costa's Intelligent Behaviors** Persistency Quality Decrease impulsivity Metacognition Accuracy Applying to past knowledge **Authentic Assessment** Performance Feedback	**Physical Environment** Yuk Spots Bright Spots Climate Goals **Affective Domain** Self-Awareness Self-Regulation Emotions Self Efficacy Empathy Attitude **Cognitive Domain** Level of Concern Risk Taking Motivation Withitness **Behavioral Expectations** **Constructive Feedback** Celebrate successes	**Information Gathering** **Discovering Self through the Researchers** Gardner Gregorc Kolb Goleman Sternberg DeBono **Self Assessment** True Colors Objects Animal Eyes **The Learner's Ways of Knowing** Surveys Inventories Questionnaires **Knowing the Learners Ways to Comprehend and Read Orally**	**Assessing Before the learning** Observations Response Cards Four Corners Surveys Questionnaires Pre-test Development Brainstorming Pre-Test **Personalizing the plan** Standards Knowledge base Ability Attitudes Interests **Assessment During the Learning** Baggie Tools Note taking Color coding Self-Talk Gathering the Data	**Questioning Techniques** Open-ended Bloom's Lead-ins **Gathering and Documentation** Observations Tallies Bus Stop Center ELOs Anecdotal Records **More Instruments and Tools** Likert Scales Rubrics Checklists Manipulatives Journals Graphic Organizers **Performance Assessment** **Teacher Made Tests** **Portfolios** **Standardized Testing** **Grading** **Conferencing**	**Learning Dispositions** Process Product Content **Planning Tools** Agendas Cubing Choice Boards Centers Labs Stations **Differentiated Models** Curriculum Compacting Contracts Project-based Model Problem Based Model **Flexible Grouping** T Total Group A Alone P Partner S Small Group **Adjustable Assignment Model** **Planning Grid** **Role of Assessment in Planning** **Differentiated Assessment Dozen**

Here is another scenario that emphasizes how differentiated assessment is essential as a guide for instructional plans. Visualize a set of gears turning a large wheel attached to smaller wheels. The speed of the major wheel determines the speed of all adjacent wheels. In a typical lesson, the teacher sets the lesson's pace to match the ability of the largest group. The other groups strive to maintain the same pace. The teacher may turn up the lesson pace for some segments and slow down for others. Students who have a broad knowledge base related to the topic are prepared to excel in their learning, but they are held back. Students who require a basic understanding of the skill or concept are pulled along and bypass the foundational or basic information they need to build future skills.

> *Our differences are unique treasures.*
>
> —Mattie Stepanek
> (2002) (age 12)

When lessons are planned for the middle group, the information is frustrating to students who need information clarified or background details magnified. Conversely, these lessons are boring and a waste of valuable time for students on the high end of learning who know the basic information and are ready to accelerate their learning. Successful teachers are aware of the detrimental effects of planning and teaching to the middle group. They use assessment data to design a rich, rigorous, differentiated curriculum to meet the needs of individual learners.

The Benefits of Ongoing Differentiated Assessment

Ongoing assessment occurs before, during, and after lessons or assignments to meet the needs of individual students. It is designed or selected to acquire information in daily activities and to provide experiences to expedite learning. Students receive regular feedback on their performances to continually improve in areas of strength and need.

An assessment may indicate that students need explicit instruction, review, or reteaching. It may point to the necessity of presenting the information or skill with a new or different approach. Individuals benefit when the teacher intervenes with assistance as soon as a need is recognized (see Table 0.1). It is important for students to know that the teacher is continually monitoring their strengths and needs to help them grow both personally and as learners.

Using Differentiated Assessment to Determine Mastery

Use of a checklist to assess a student's mastery of a skill, standard, or objective is a common teaching practice. The teacher places a check mark

Table 0.1   Cognitive and Affective Benefits of Ongoing Differentiated Assessment

Cognitive Benefits	Affective Benefits
• Uses assessment data to intervene and avoid gaps in learning • Reduces failure • Challenges within the learner's level of success • Increases time on-task • Builds on the learner's knowledge base, experiences, and ability • Accelerates learning	• Encourages and empowers • Provides security • Supports risk taking • Uses mistakes as positive learning opportunities • Creates bonds • Reduces frustration • Develops confidence • Generates self-motivation

beside the item on a list to indicate minimum competence if the student uses the information or skill correctly. Check marks indicate that the student knows the information at that specific point in time, but the student may be unable to recall or apply it later. When true mastery is achieved, the student can prove competency by automatically applying the learning after several days have passed.

Think about mastery of a concept by visualizing a dart-throwing contest. A contestant hits the bull's-eye on the first three throws. This demonstrates dart-throwing competence. It is obvious that this individual has mastered the skill. The second contestant hits the bull's-eye one or two times out of three tries. This individual is still in a hit-or-miss mode and has not yet achieved mastery. Keep the bull's-eye metaphor in mind as you assess a student's mastery of standards or skills. Provide opportunities for the student to demonstrate two to three times that he or she knows how to use the information immediately and effectively in various circumstances.

Beware of drawing conclusions related to mastery. When a skill or a piece of factual information is taught, the student may use it correctly following the lesson. Remember, true mastery is evident when the student uses the skill automatically after several days have passed.

WHAT IS THE TEACHER'S ROLE IN DIFFERENTIATED ASSESSMENT?

According to the *Webster's New World College Dictionary* (2001), the word *assessment* means "appraisal." It is derived from the Latin word *assidere,* which means "to sit beside." In an ideal situation, the teacher sits beside the student during the assessment activity to provide support and immediate feedback. The learner receives instruction in each skill as a need evolves. It is physically impossible to sit beside each student during each assessment. However, it is possible for each student to feel that the teacher is his or her personal coach and cheerleader. All learners need to know the teacher is there as a guide to provide assistance, praise, encouragement, and high expectations.

Teachers are required to follow mandated state standards, benchmarks, essential questions, or indicators. In most cases, they have the autonomy to choose the resources, techniques, and appropriate times to teach the required skills. When assessment experiences are orchestrated with intriguing tools and strategies, opportunities are created to open doors to learning.

The teacher's task is to differentiate assessment experiences using various amounts of the following:

- Content
- Resources
- Tools
- Formats

- Tasks
- Strategies
- Feedback techniques
- Performances

The teacher uses results from a variety of assessment experiences to determine students' achievement levels. Students have opportunities to demonstrate that they have the appropriate background, know the information, and are ready for the next step.

Assessment data is used to determine if learners need more work on particular skills or if they are ready to move on to new skills. These critical, decision-making assessment experiences are discussed throughout this book.

> *While the evaluation process depends on assessment, assessment is only the first step in the evaluation process. Data, by itself—without observational components and interpretation—has no meaningful place in instruction or informed teaching. You can't make a value judgment about test scores; they are merely raw data. It's the interpretation of that data which brings one to the evaluation level. (Routman, 2002)*

Why Are Differentiated Assessment Tools Essential?

Differentiated assessment tools are selected or designed to provide the complete picture of students' needs. Keep in mind that the goal of each assessment experience is to show what the learner needs to know and to improve his or her ability to master new skills and strategies.

Differentiated assessment tools are needed to gather information about students because each individual is unique in the following ways:

- Knowledge base
- Prior experiences and background
- Motivation
- Attitude toward the topic or subject

- Emotions and desires
- Learning styles and modalities
- Multiple intelligences
- Abilities, interests, and talents

Differentiated assessment accelerates the student's ability to learn new information, facts, skills, or concepts. The results of an assessment activity reveal the student's specific needs and strengths. This data guides the teacher in making instructional decisions for each student. When the results are analyzed, the teacher considers appropriate options, including the following:

1. Provide more *in-depth* instruction.

2. Revisit previous lessons.

3. Move to the next step.

4. Create specific plans.

5. Engage learners in areas of enrichment or personal interest through choice selections.

The Benefits of Differentiated Assessment Strategies

Students and teachers benefit from differentiated assessment because data gathered from various sources provide a metaphoric mosaic of each student's readiness for learning specific skills or topics. The mosaic artwork is complete when each piece is in place to complete a design. Some mosaics are created from a multitude of small pieces, whereas others comprise large puzzle pieces. In a similar way, various pieces of assessment data are needed to form a complete picture of the unique needs of a student.

One standard may require detailed assessment data to complete the whole picture. In another case, a quick observation of students may provide adequate assessment data to use in planning because students need only one or two pieces of the puzzle. If the standard is composed of complex thinking processes, it may require multiple assessments to complete a total, in-depth view of the student. The teacher and student benefit when they work together to make all the pieces fit.

In a differentiated classroom, the teacher provides opportunities for all students to use higher-order thinking skills. Too often, students who excel are the only learners who are presented with these tasks. Those who have difficulty learning are too often given basic, rote assignments and assessments. All students benefit when they are challenged with essential skills, questions, processes, and ideas to learn within their personal levels of understanding.

Taking the Initial Steps

Take Small Steps Into Differentiated Assessment

When using this resource independently, teachers need to proceed incrementally because it contains a vast treasure trove of ongoing assessment ideas. Anyone approaching differentiated instruction and assessment for the first time is advised to choose one or two favorite strategies for implementation. For example, start by giving students choices. Begin on a limited basis and expand your use of the tools as you grow more comfortable. On a unit test, a teacher might allow students to choose how they want to show their understanding of the water cycle. The options may include writing a description by drawing the process or labeling appropriate transitions and phases. Gradually expand the kinds of assessment choices you offer students as you work with this powerful strategy. Next, add self-talk or cubing and again work with each one until it feels natural. As the benefits are reaped, dip back into this resource to expand your repertoire.

Use Differentiated Assessment Tools as Job-Embedded Experiences

Staff developers and administrators will find that the differentiated assessment activities and strategies may be presented to teachers as job-embedded experiences. This involves on-site demonstrations for careful selection of the tools or approaches that meet the diverse needs of an individual or group of students. To accomplish this rewarding task, grade-level teams or colleague partners may take a section or chapter of the book and present specific assessment tools through exhibits and role-playing. It is important that the follow-up activities include an analysis and discussion of practical ways to adapt the identified tools.

The goal is for the participants to become familiar with the strategies as practical, carry-to-the-classroom tools. Remind them to adapt each strategy to their content area and their individual or group needs. Provide opportunities for teachers to share and celebrate their experiences with the various assessment tools.

Opening the Toolbox

The teacher designs adjustable assignments by using the appropriate assessment tools to identify the learner's knowledge base and prior experiences related to a standard, topic, or skill. The information gathered provides a guide for instruction, so each student can begin on his or her level of understanding and grow during the learning process. A student's entry point for instruction is identified through the differentiated assessment data to provide the most productive learning opportunities.

Practical applications of the research presented here are found in the various strategies and activities presented throughout the book. More research is embedded in the methods, models, and approaches to differentiated assessment.

We hope educators use these differentiated assessment tools to personalize assessment experiences. We designed or selected the numerous strategies, activities, and ideas so teachers can strategically use each one as a differentiated assessment tool because . . .

> *One tool doesn't fit all.*
>
> —Chapman and King

**CORWIN
PRESS**

The Corwin Press logo—a raven striding across an open book—represents the union of courage and learning. Corwin Press is committed to improving education for all learners by publishing books and other professional development resources for those serving the field of K–12 education. By providing practical, hands-on materials, Corwin Press continues to carry out the promise of its motto: **"Helping Educators Do Their Work Better."**

Bringing Brain Research Into Practice With Differentiated Assessment

1

Essential Question: How can brain research be used to enhance and customize assessment experiences to make them personally meaningful for diverse learners?

The strategies, activities, and suggestions in this resource are based on recent brain research and effective learning and assessment techniques. The following section presents an overview of theories, effective practices, and current research that influences and guides our work with differentiated assessment. Use these ideas to apply the research to the data-gathering process.

INFORMATION PROCESSING AND MEMORY

It is important for teachers to understand how basic brain functions relate to information processing to improve each learner's assessment experiences. In *How the Brain Learns*, David Sousa (2001) explains that during each experience and learning activity, the brain scans incoming information. The sensory register analyzes it and acts as a guard, to turn it away or to admit it, based in part on past experience with related input. If the information is determined to be nonthreatening or insignificant, it may be discarded. If deemed to be important, valuable, or meaningful, the information enters the working memory. Keep in mind that the student, not the teacher, determines the importance, value, or need. Even for the student, this determination is partially unconscious.

Mel Levine (2002), a pediatrician and learning expert, states that a student may have difficulty deciding what is important. If a learner does not possess an effective filtering system, his or her brain takes in worthless or useless information. Another student may receive the important information but be unable to focus on specific segments of it. Teachers must explicitly model how to identify valuable information.

If the student focuses, or pays attention, the brain transfers the information into working memory. Here the brain combines new and old learning and manipulates the pieces to create understanding. In this processing stage, the information is prepared for immediate use or storage in long-term memory.

Students need to know how to develop their ability to retain information. This too must be explicitly taught in daily activities. For instance, learners need to know the role of focused attention in activating the brain and opening the gateways to memory. They need to be familiar with strategies that connect prior experiences, attach meaning, and prepare information for long-term storage. This is accomplished by working with the information, organizing the facts or ideas, and creating retrieval cues. When students have opportunities to thoroughly process information in working memory, they are likely to store it in ways that make retrieval easy and automatic. A learner's success with each assessment experience depends on his or her memory skills and ability to retrieve the requested information.

Why Students Forget and Why They Remember

Following an assessment, teachers often say, "I just taught this information; I can't believe they didn't remember it!" Dempster and Corkill, (1999) identified several factors that interfere with memory. Table 1.1 presents practical interpretations of these factors and provides some possible solutions for each one.

ASSIST THE BRAIN IN MEMORY PROCESSING

Working memory is the thinking or processing stage of learning. To help students process information in working memory, present strategies that

Table 1.1   Why Students Forget and Why They Remember

Why Students Forget	What Does It Mean?	Memory Solutions
Interference	• New information and thoughts block concentration.	• Teach attention strategies • Use intriguing activities • Remove distractions • Provide attention prompts
Retroactive Inhibition	• Two or more similar bits of information enter the brain at the same time.	• Teach similar pieces of information separately and thoroughly using different strategies • Present distinguishing examples or steps
Proactive Inhibition	• Previously learned information interferes with new learning. • The information or skill did not have distinguishing features or characteristics.	• Provide detailed attributes or discriptors • Create buy-in to the value of the new information • Apply the new information to the learner's world
Cue Dependent Forgetting	• The retrieval cue was not a meaningful hook for the information. • The memory tool was not rehearsed.	• Overlearn mnemonic techniques • Practice for automaticity
Decay Theory	• The information was not used. • "If you don't use it, you lose it!"	• Apply it • Practice • Review • Use it in new situations

give the brain opportunities to work with new information. Use the following guidelines to present new topic and skills. The term *assessment* is the new topic in the following examples. Create examples for your topics of study from the italicized list of categories to assist the learners as they mentally manipulate and process new terms.

Make Personal Connections

Discuss ways students observe or apply _____ in their everyday activities. This provides personal connections and associations with the term and makes students more conscious of the benefit and frequency of its use in their present and future lives.

Choose one or two topics from the following list to introduce and explain to students how assessment is experienced in their daily activities:

After school a student uses assessment when he or she . . .

- Uses a taste test to select a favorite ice cream flavor
- Looks over clothes in the closet to select an outfit for the day
- Chooses the best seat in a movie theater

At school a student experiences assessment when he or she . . .

- Receives a grade for an assignment
- Auditions for cheerleading or a role in a play
- Is selecting the best way to present a report

In the workplace, assessment is used when . . .

- The dentist decides on the best way to repair a tooth
- A cook chooses the best spices to improve the taste of a new dish
- A doctor selects the most effective prescription for the diagnosis

After an introduction, challenge students to identify additional ways they use assessment in their daily activities. Create a class list on a chart or poster by compiling the responses.

Project the Value of the New Information

- This information will be valuable to you when . . .
- When you know how to use assessment tools automatically, you will be able to . . .

Organize and Categorize the Facts, Thoughts, and Ideas

- List the various ways you use assessment in daily activities.
- Write the steps to the assessment activity in sequential order.

Make Connections to Prior Knowledge and Experiences

- How have you used assessment in the past?
- How has assessment guided you to improve a skill?

Analyze the Component

- Examine each step of the assessment activity.
- Explain each component of the assessment tool in your own words.

Summarize the Component

- Explain all of the steps used with the assessment tool in a nutshell or a brief paragraph.
- What are the essential features of the assessment strategy?

Evaluate the Component

- How is assessment valuable in the work of someone you know?
- How useful will assessment be to you throughout your years in school?

Apply Memory Strategies to Create Retrieval Cues

- Design a mnemonic strategy to record and remember assessment facts.
- Create a song, rap, jingle, or poem to remember the terms related to assessment.

A student's success with each standard and skill depends on his or her ability to process, record, and apply information in the required format. Provide experiences that incorporate these ideas to optimize learning and enhance assessment activities.

Transfer

Transfer is a term used to describe the student's ability to learn new information and apply it in a new situation (Bransford, Brown, & Cocking, 1999). A major goal of instruction is to show the learner how to apply facts, skills, or ideas in different ways after some time has elapsed. Students need to understand that information that does not result in transfer has as much value as water poured on a duck's back. Effective teachers plan instruction for automatic transfer of information and skills to similar and new situations.

The ability to use new knowledge is the learner's key to success. Assessments reveal the student's ability to apply or transfer knowledge.

Students are more likely to transfer learned information, skills, and ideas to assessment activities when the teacher does the following:

- Creates meaningful experiences for the student
- Uses terms that are easy for the student to understand and apply
- Provides examples that relate to their world
- Makes understanding the focus of teaching and learning
- Guides students to apply new learning to other academic areas and to their daily activities
- Uses a variety of differentiated assessment tools for simulations, demonstrations, and performances that allow students to practice using their unique knowledge of facts, skills, or ideas

Novelty

Novelty is anything new, different, or unique that captures the mind's attention. According to David Sousa (2001), the brain is continually alert and responding to stimuli in the environment. Take advantage of this phenomenon to focus and maintain the student's attention. Use novel strategies, such as the following examples, to build anticipation and create curiosity to enhance instruction and assessment experiences:

- Model and practice with an intriguing variety of memory strategies and retrieval cues.
- Employ flexible grouping scenarios.
- Use a variety of formats, materials, and tools.
- Present with effective hooks.
- Use intriguing problem-solving experiences to stretch the mind.

Automaticity

Automaticity is the student's ability to easily access and immediately apply information stored in memory. As individuals learn and practice a new skill, they become more efficient (Eden et al., 1996). When students quickly and correctly apply information as needed, true automaticity is demonstrated. An example of automaticity is evident in first draft writing. If students use correct punctuation as they answer open-ended questions on a written test, complete a first-draft writing assignment, or write a note to a friend, mastery of punctuation is evident.

If you ask students to demonstrate the same knowledge the following week, they may not recall the information. If this occurs, the skill or information was learned for the moment, not for long-term application or lifetime use. True mastery is demonstrated when students transfer the knowledge correctly and automatically in various situations after several days or weeks have passed. Establish automaticity as the goal for mastery of each assessed skill and strategy.

DEVELOP INTELLIGENT BEHAVIORS FOR ASSESSMENT

In his book *The School as a Home for the Mind*, Art Costa (1991) presents a list of characteristics that reflect intelligent behaviors. Students who consistently receive high assessment scores usually exhibit these behaviors.

Foster Intelligent Behaviors During Assessment Experiences

It is important to incorporate intelligent behaviors in daily lessons and routines to empower learners during assessments. In the following section, the authors selected six intelligent behaviors and applied them to assessment. Explanations for these behaviors are presented with suggestions and ideas for use with students. Use the sayings on banners and posters or use them in raps or jingles to reinforce the behaviors.

Persistence

Persistence is an individual's desire to continue his efforts to complete a task. Create assessments that provide opportunities for success. Teach each student within his or her Zone of Proximal Development. This zone is the level where the student is capable of learning with some assistance (Vygotsky, 1978). In this learning stage, the student does not feel too bored or too challenged. Reward a student's efforts with specific, genuine praise.

> *Winners never quit.*

Share examples of persistence in the lives of famous heroes, role models, and champions.

Abraham Lincoln	Michael Jordan	Lance Armstrong
Helen Keller	Mary Kay	Margaret Thatcher

Quality

Emphasize and praise the *quality*, not the quantity or amount of the student's work. Show students how to do the following:

- Identify quality or what is important, such as setting obtainable priorities and goals
- Analyze materials and distinguish between the least and most valuable items
- Practice selective abandonment

Demonstrate the following examples of self-talk as praise statements for quality work habits:

- Wow! I did a great job on that problem.
- Yes! I completed my assignment correctly.
- I am proud of myself because I . . .

> *Be the best that you can be!*

Decrease Impulsivity

The impulsive learner often acts without thinking, so he or she becomes careless with assessment activities. This student needs to see the value of thinking through his or her own actions and decisions. Remind the learner that spontaneity is an advantage in many situations, but impulsivity often becomes detrimental during assessments.

> *Haste Maketh Waste!*
>
> —John Heywood

Share the fable *The Tortoise and the Hare*. Discuss the lesson reflected in the turtle's steadfast determination and consistent movement toward his goal. Identify and model the steps students use to process, retrieve, review, and check information during assessments.

Metacognition

Teach the value of metacognition, or "thinking about thinking." Model self-talk strategies the learner can use to activate metacognition (see Chapter 4). Remember, it takes time to think.

The following are examples of self-talk to prompt metacognition during assessment:

> *I think about my thinking!*

- How do I solve this problem?
- Can I repeat the directions?
- Am I following the correct sequence or procedure?
- I'll check my work to see if I followed the rules.
- Is there a better way to complete this task?
- What steps did I use to complete the problem?

Striving for Accuracy and Precision

Teach skills that eliminate incorrect responses. Model easy steps to follow while checking work. For example, after a student completes an addition problem by adding from top to bottom, demonstrate how to check it by adding from bottom to top.

Emphasize the value of reading directions thoroughly before beginning tasks in daily work and assessments. The following activity can be adapted to all subjects and grade levels.

Activity: Following Directions

In the following activity it becomes clear to learners that they need to read and follow the directions. When students "read all directions before beginning," they see that instruction number 5 tells them not to complete the first four directions. The only items to complete are numbers 6 and 7.

Read all directions before beginning the following activity. Work until you hear a signal to stop.

1. Draw a square.

2. Divide the square into four smaller squares.

3. Draw a diagonal line in each small square to create two right-triangles.

4. Draw a star in each right triangle.

5. Continue to work quietly, but do not complete the previous directions for numbers 1 through 4.

6. Make a list of your favorite books, movies, foods, or television shows until the teacher gives the signal to stop.

7. Stand up. Pat yourself on the back and say *"yes!"* if you read all directions first.

Note: This activity illustrates the value of reading all directions before beginning an activity. Students "get" this message and enjoy similar activities.

A Stitch in Time Saves Nine.

Applying Past Knowledge to New Situations

Refer to the student's past and current knowledge to make meaningful connections to the new skill or strategy. Find out as much as you can about his or her experiences, attitude, and background in relation to a topic. These factors have a major impact on learning. Create opportunities for the student to recall past experiences. Explain many ways to activate prior knowledge and build on personal experiences to make mental connections to new facts or ideas.

Examples: Applying Past Knowledge to New Situations

Write about it.

- Draw a cartoon that illustrates your knowledge.
- Discuss with a partner how your experiences or knowledge relate to the new information.
- Create a rap to describe how your past experiences can be used with the new skill.
- Preassess prior experiences using surveys, inventories, and questions.

Use self-talk to activate memory of prior knowledge and experiences.

- Where have I heard about this skill or strategy before?
- How have I used this information in the past?
- How can I use what I know to work with the new information?

AUTHENTIC ASSESSMENT

Authentic assessment presents activities that give learners opportunities to use information or skills in realistic situations (Campbell, 2000). This alternative to formal and standardized testing is recognized as providing the best evidence of learning because students must show that they can use the information or skill. The teacher designs authentic assessment activities and experiences by engaging students in tasks that simulate life experiences.

Use a variety of authentic assessment tools that allow students to demonstrate their abilities to process and apply information, skills, and concepts in different ways. Model how to use each tool so students understand and know how to apply it. Remember, students are more likely to store information when they have opportunities to use it in personal, meaningful ways.

Teachers and those who support instruction need to know when and how to use all assessment tools available to them. In his book *Student-Involved Classroom Assessment*, R. J. Stiggins (2001) advocates a balanced perspective with respect to the use of assessment methods. Stiggins suggests the use of selected student-response formats, essay assessment, performance assessment, and personal communication with students. He asserts that none of these alternatives is inherently more or less powerful or appropriate than other approaches. Each can serve well when developed and implemented in the right context by informed users. Table 1.2 identifies some of the distinguishing characteristics of traditional and authentic approaches to assessment.

Grant Wiggins (1993), an expert in the field of educational assessment, affirms that authentic assessment should be a "direct examination of student performance on worthy intellectual tasks." His research suggests that student assessment must be built on the following:

- Criteria regarding the expected types of behaviors or attributes of a product
- A well-defined scoring system for evaluation

According to Wiggins, authentic assessment does the following:

- Offers students a variety of tasks using acquired knowledge and real-life skills, such as collaboration, research, writing, revising, and discussing
- Assists in discovering whether students can create valid answers, performances, or products
- Standardizes criteria to achieve validity and reliability for scoring student projects
- Guides students to rehearse for authentic roles in adult life

Table 1.2 View of Traditional and Authentic Assessment

Traditional	Authentic
• Short answers • Paper • Workbook • Pen and pencil • Easy to administer • Quick, easy grading • Specific time limits • Reflects recall ability	• Application to real-life situations • Hands-on activities • Multiple skills in a task • Demonstrations of ability to apply information • Ongoing for days, weeks, or throughout a unit of study • Reflects growth in a skill or ability

Performance Feedback

Performance feedback has been emphasized in the results of numerous studies as a technique to enhance student achievement. Hattie (1996) analyzed over a thousand studies on effective teaching. He concluded that feedback is a powerful learning strategy. According to Marzano, Pickering, and Pollock (2001), when corrective feedback is presented in a timely manner, students have great opportunities to improve. Differentiated assessment is designed to provide students with the specific feedback and guidance they need to be successful in daily activities and assignments.

> *Appropriate, ongoing assessment keeps the learner on track in the learning journey.*
>
> —Chapman and King

Ongoing differentiated assessment assists students as their needs occur in daily activities. Individuals receive prompt interventions with specific, corrective feedback as they work. This avoids the pitfalls of failure as students learn to monitor their own work and take more personal control of learning.

Creating a 2 Climate for Assessment

Essential Question: How is the classroom environment designed to create a positive learning climate during each differentiated assessment experience?

When a positive climate is evident in a classroom, each person knows he or she belongs to a learning community. This culture is reflected in the look and feel of the classroom. In this environment, students know they are valued team members.

In an effective classroom, students view each assessment activity as a way to highlight their strengths and needs so they can improve, extend, and celebrate learning. In other words, each assessment is approached as a productive experience.

Teachers must continually monitor the classroom to find ways to optimize the assessment environment to meet each student's cognitive and affective needs. The general climate has a direct impact on the learner's success. The physical environment has a positive or negative effect on students' assessment experiences. It is made up of the type of seats, the furniture arrangement, visuals, lighting, air quality, and temperature. It also includes objects in the immediate vicinity and the peripherals, or visible surroundings. Everything within the learners' vicinity plays a major role in the climate and affects the student-environment fit.

Activity: Yuk Spots/Bright Spots Scavenger Hunt

This activity is designed for teachers and students to identify physical aspects of the classroom or work areas that need to be improved or maintained. Places or things that need to be improved are the *Yuk Spots*. The areas that need to be maintained are the *Bright Spots*.

1. Create teams, and ask each group to choose a name for their team.
2. Tell each team to select a captain and a recorder.
   a. Captain's role: Rally the team together and lead discussions.
   b. Recorder's role: Record findings for the team during the activity.
3. Send the teams on a tour of classrooms or work areas. If needed, set time limits.
4. Ask each team to follow the directions for Yuk Spots and Bright Spots on the charts provided (see Figures 2.1, 2.2, and 2.3).

Yuk Spots: Directions

When a team member finds something that needs to be repaired or improved in the school's physical setting, the recorder lists it as a Yuk Spot in the first column under "What is it?" and then completes the column "Where is it?" The team then decides if a short-term or long-term goal is needed to correct or improve it. If an identified Yuk Spot can be fixed within a brief period of time with a minimum amount of labor and effort, it is listed as a short-term goal. Action is taken immediately to take care of these needs. If it is costly, takes an extended amount of time, or requires extensive manpower, it is recorded as a long-term goal. These needs are placed in an implementation plan with a timeline.

Talk with the teams about how some Yuk Spots must be addressed by administrators or staff members. These areas can still be identified with suggested action steps. The list may be sent to the principal or board to request specific improvements and volunteer assistance.

Bright Spots: Directions

Identify Bright Spots in the hallways, classrooms, or work areas. These are the existing places and spaces that brighten, enhance, and support a positive learning environment. As each Bright Spot is discovered on the team's tour, the recorder lists each one in the column "What is it?" and then gives the location in the column "Where is it?" The remaining columns, "Why do we need to keep it?" and "Are there any changes needed?" are completed with brainstormed responses.

Setting Climate Goals

After assessing the climate, look at specific areas of need. Set goals and establish a plan for improvement (see Table 2.1). Remember, short-term goals are easier to obtain, so address these plans first. When everyone

(*Text continues on page 18*)

Figure 2.1   Yuk Spots

Identify the Yuk Spots in the hallways, classrooms, or work areas that need to be improved to enhance the environment. Record the team members' comments and ideas related to each area.

What is it?	Where is it?	Short-term goal Action steps	Long-term goal Action steps

Team Name: _____

Captain's Name: _____

Recorder's Name: _____

Names of team members: _____

_____

Date of tour: _____

Figure 2.2   Bright Spots

Identify the Bright Spots in the hallways, classrooms, or work areas that enhance the environment. Record the team members' comments and ideas related to each area.

What is it?	Where is it?	Why do we need to keep it?	Are any changes needed?

Team Name: _____

Captain's Name: _____

Recorder's Name: _____

Names of team members: _____

_____

Date of tour: _____

Figure 2.3   Teacher Assessment of the Classroom Environment

The environment will strongly benefit from the teacher's evaluation, too. Aspects for scrutiny should include the physical environment but extend to deeper realms of learner support as well. The following chart may be adapted to analyze the learning environment for assessment experiences. Check the appropriate boxes.

Teacher _____   Class _____   Date _____

	Rarely	Sometimes	Often	Most of the time
Students are . . .				
1. Given time to think.	☐	☐	☐	☐
2. Encouraged to take risks.	☐	☐	☐	☐
3. Becoming self-directed learners.	☐	☐	☐	☐
4. Comfortable when asking and answering questions.	☐	☐	☐	☐
5. Learning from mistakes and accomplishments.	☐	☐	☐	☐
6. Aware that learning is acquired by building on prior experiences and background knowledge.	☐	☐	☐	☐
7. Given opportunities to learn from others and to work alone.	☐	☐	☐	☐
8. Helped to see mistakes as learning experiences.	☐	☐	☐	☐
9. Treated with respect.	☐	☐	☐	☐
10. Given specific praise.	☐	☐	☐	☐
11. Honored for their efforts, strengths, and talents.	☐	☐	☐	☐
12. Valued as members of the learning community.	☐	☐	☐	☐
The physical arrangement of the classroom . . .				
1. Promotes learning.	☐	☐	☐	☐
2. Permits flexible grouping for assessment.	☐	☐	☐	☐
3. Is customized to meet the learners' assessment needs.	☐	☐	☐	☐
4. Is conducive to productive experiences.	☐	☐	☐	☐
5. Is inviting and comfortable.	☐	☐	☐	☐
6. Accommodates personal needs.	☐	☐	☐	☐
7. Honors diversity.	☐	☐	☐	☐
The classroom visuals . . .				
1. Are samples of student work.	☐	☐	☐	☐
2. Reflect student learning.	☐	☐	☐	☐
3. Showcase the learners' strengths and growth.	☐	☐	☐	☐
4. Are novel, effective learning tools.	☐	☐	☐	☐
5. Are displayed at students' eye levels.	☐	☐	☐	☐
6. Contain assessment reminders and tips.	☐	☐	☐	☐
7. Correlate with the current topic or unit of study.	☐	☐	☐	☐
8. Are student centered.	☐	☐	☐	☐
9. Celebrate success with assessment activities.	☐	☐	☐	☐

Variation: Ask students to complete the above checklist to see how they view the classroom's climate. Combine the teacher and student responses to improve the classroom's learning culture.

Table 2.1   Climate Goals: An Implementation Grid

Goal	Procedures/Actions for Implementation	Progress Notes
1.		
2.		
3.		

sees immediate improvements in the learning environment, feelings of accomplishment are exhilarating.

Think about the learning climate in which most assessments are administered. Did *positive testing environment* come to mind? To some, this phrase qualifies as an oxymoron because the words *positive* and *testing* are usually incompatible. An air of negativity often surrounds most assessment scenes. Because the brain functions best in a stimulating and psychologically safe environment, negativity must be eliminated. Present each formal and informal assessment experience in a relaxed atmosphere where high expectations are evident without creating undue stress and anxiety.

The climate has a major influence on the learners' motivation and success with the assessment experiences. In an effective classroom, all aspects of the environment promote learning during instruction and assessment activities.

THE AFFECTIVE DOMAIN AND ASSESSMENT

The affective domain of teaching and learning includes all areas that influence students' emotions, including their mind-sets, levels of interest, and motivations. Negative feelings create barriers to success, so it is imperative for the teacher to maintain a positive, comfortable, and inviting assessment environment.

> [T]he skill in good teaching lies in the capacity to orchestrate the sensory context of the class. (Caine & Caine, 1994)

Students' perceptions of the classroom climate are affected by the teacher's presence and personal interactions. Voice tone, high expectations, energy, enthusiasm, and genuine interest are key elements in the classroom's assessment atmosphere. The teacher continually monitors the affective aspects of the environment to assure student success. For example, it is important to promptly recognize the telltale signs of confusion or frustration so reteaching or clarification can remove these barriers to learning.

One incident can instantaneously change a student's attitude from positive to negative, so his or her feelings must be monitored. The teacher must be consciously aware of how his or her words and body language are perceived, especially when identifying student errors in assessment feedback. When the teacher is aware of a student's negative feelings, a positive attitude can be reestablished for optimal learning.

The affective assessment climate is reflected in the student's desire to grow in understanding. This is evident when someone in class exclaims "I got it!" "Let me show you how I figured it out a different way," or "Help me, I don't understand this at all." In the last example, the student is seeking assistance from classmates or the teacher, and in this atmosphere the student knows he or she will receive help to improve in a specific skill or area of knowledge.

Emotions

An emotionally safe environment plays a major role in the brain's level of functioning during assessment activities. If an individual has unpleasant memories or experiences with a topic, subject, teacher, or classroom design, these internal feelings create barriers to, or interfere with, learning and assessment. If a student has pleasant, stimulating learning adventures related to the topic, subject, teacher, or classroom, his or her mind becomes an open vessel for new learning. This student is eager to show what he or she knows. Remember, this attitude may change quickly if the new experiences become negative or unchallenging.

> *Emotion is our biological thermostat and is thus central to cognition and educational practice. (Sylwester, 2000)*

Pay close attention to the emotions tied to the assessment. If the student has negative vibes, this can cause the experience to be a simple walk-through, as the learner merely goes through the motions. Negative emotions often block or interfere with the mental pathways that lead to memory. If the student is emotionally and academically prepared for the assessment experience, he or she is more able to link, retrieve, and apply previously learned information and skills.

Emotional Intelligence

The work of Daniel Goleman (1995, 1998) on emotional intelligence applies to differentiated assessment. Goleman describes the intellect as working "in concert" with the emotions. The gamut of emotions is evident in assessment activities: anxiety, frustration, dread, disappointment, embarrassment, pride, pleasure, and exhilaration.

The following list contains the emotional intelligences as defined by Goleman. The authors have added the indicator examples that may be shared with students. Strategically plan learning and assessment activities to foster these characteristics:

Self-awareness

- Understands feelings
- Knows strengths and needs
- Possesses self-confidence

Self-regulation

- Delays gratification to pursue goals
- Works to complete personal and academic tasks
- Possesses the ability to recover from setbacks

Motivation

- Shows initiative
- Has an innate desire to improve
- Keeps trying after failure

Empathy

- Feels what others are feeling
- Respects diverse views of other individuals
- Is loyal and supportive

Social skills

- Is a vital team member
- Communicates effectively with verbals and nonverbals
- Gets along with others
- Learns during partner and group work

Risk Taking as Emotional Bravery

Explain to students that risk-taking experiences can lead to uncomfortable, unknown territory or knowledge. They need to know that each risk requires emotional bravery. Inform students that their efforts may result in errors or mistakes that may leave them open to negative comments or may bring successes and result in celebrations. Remind everyone that bravery produces good feelings. Model the risk-taking strategies needed for success with assessment tasks. For example, demonstrate the value of guessing. Making an educated or "smart" guess is an example of this behavior and reflects individual persistence. Make students feel good about guessing or trying to find the answer so they put forth this effort in future activities. Each risk deserves praise. Teach self-talk techniques for risk taking, as in the following examples:

I give myself a pat on the back because I tried!

I am proud of myself because I always do my best.

Remember, self-confidence and the desire to improve are prerequisites for taking risks. Maintain a classroom atmosphere that promotes individual risk taking as a valuable assessment skill.

SELF-EFFICACY

Self-efficacy is the student's belief in himself or herself and in his or her ability to succeed. Students' self-perceptions are influenced by the teacher's comments and reactions related to their tasks and their performance of a task (Bandura, 1997). Self-efficacy plays a major role in the learner's efforts during assessment experiences. When the student believes it is possible to reach the expected level of mastery, he or she will try. However, if the student feels inadequate, he or she will exhibit little or no effort. Therefore, one of the best ways to develop self-efficacy is to design assessment tasks on the student's success level.

Post slogans in the classroom that are similar to the following to promote self-efficacy:

I believe in ME!

I will . . . I will . . . I will ZAP the GAPS!

I am a success because I do my best!

Each comment and gesture by the teacher reflects his or her feelings and attitudes related to assessment. The teacher's body language and verbal innuendos have a significant impact on the way learners respond to assessments. These feelings leave impressions that endure for a lifetime.

Negative Teacher Messages

We have to complete this assessment. We don't have a choice.

I don't want to do this either.

We can _____ as soon as we finish.

Positive Teacher Messages

Show how much you've learned!

I am anxious to see your answers!

Show your best work!

Attitude Is Altitude!

Post and discuss this phrase for everyone to view daily.

This mind-set has to be present for the teacher and learners to reach their potentials. If learning is to take place, the teacher must present the material in a way that "hooks" students and keeps them focused. To develop a positive attitude about learning, students must believe they need the information and that it is relevant to their lives.

Each lesson has the potential to turn a student on or off to future learning experiences. As information enters the brain, a student unconsciously, but automatically, analyzes it. The student's emotions produce thoughts that automatically open or close the gateways to memory. Examine the following sample statements that may open or close gateways to memory:

Closing the Mind

I can't use this information.

This does not apply to me.

This is not for me.

I don't like this!

Opening the Mind

I can use this information when I _____.

I remember _____ from _____.

This is exactly what I needed to know.

Wow! This is going to be interesting.

MOTIVATION FOR ASSESSMENT

Intrinsic motivations are internal to the learner. Interest, curiosity and challenge have been shown to promote and sustain higher levels of learning. Conversely, extrinsic motivations that are imposed externally, such as grades, recognition, and competition, focus the learner on minimal levels of task completion. (Deci, Vallerand, Pelletier, & Ryans, 1991)

A great teaching challenge is to maintain students' desires to learn. Teachers often say a student is capable but not interested in completing assessment tasks. Is it more likely that he or she may be unchallenged? Lack of engagement often occurs when there is repetition in assessment activities. When the student feels that the activity is monotonous or boring, his or her mind wanders and focuses on unrelated thoughts or events in his or her daily life. In this mental state, the learner misses vital or intriguing directions and information. The student does not automatically "turn on the switch" to examine his or her own learning or engage in an activity because the preoccupied mind does not hear the signal that an upcoming activity is meaningful or of personal interest. This state of unawareness affects a learner's cognitive growth. *The teacher holds the keys to motivation.*

Pleasure derived from effort and success is a strong, natural motivator. Assessment activities should be planned on the student's success level. When a learner's efforts are rewarded, he or she has the desire to engage in the activity again. Positive experiences generate pleasurable, intrinsic motivation.

Balance the Learner's Level of Concern

The learner's desire to succeed plays an important role in the amount of mental and physical energy he or she exerts to succeed in a task. When motivational levels are too low, a student may exhibit an "I don't care" attitude. Previous failures, boredom, peer pressure, and an unchallenged mind contribute to this state. Plan many successful experiences to raise his or her level of concern and develop an internal desire to succeed.

When expectations are too high, the student may experience stress and anxiety. This may be evident when parents and teachers place too much pressure on the learner. Sometimes this may be self-induced and result in a fear of failure. These feelings often place the student in an anxious state that interferes with thinking.

The effective teacher is aware of the student's level of concern and strategically plans to raise or lower the level of anxiety so his or her mental activity is dedicated to the assessment task. The student's level of concern fluctuates with topics, the settings, teachers, or situations in his or her personal life.

Use a continuum similar to Table 2.2 to assess the attitude and feelings of a student toward an assessment task. Number 1 on the scale represents the student who has "no desire" to work. This student's refusal to complete the assessment demonstrates a low level of concern. On the opposite end of the scale, number 8 represents the student who demonstrates "great desire," or a high level of concern. This is exhibited in the learner's strong interest to correctly complete the task.

Success breeds success. Students who experience success enjoy and receive personal satisfaction. They strive to succeed again to create the same feelings. Keep this in mind as assessment tools, strategies, and activities are selected to meet the student's productive levels of concern.

"Withitness"

Teachers and students see "withitness" slightly differently, but, by either definition, withitness contributes to teacher success. The term

Table 2.2   The Engagement-Disengagement Spectrum of Feelings and Responses

Feelings	Possible Observed Reactions
No desire to engage in assessment	
1. I am not going to do this.	Does not do it
2. I would rather not do this.	Does something else
3. I do not want to do this.	Exhibits a negative attitude
4. I'll just do the easy parts.	Completes a few parts
5. I will do enough to stay out of trouble.	Tasks are incomplete
6. I have to complete this because it is required.	Does enough to get by
7. I understand, and I am going to do this.	Completes it to the best of his or her ability
8. I am excited about doing my very best on this work.	Does the best work possible
Great desire to engage in assessment	

withitness was coined by Kounin (1970) to describe the teacher's awareness of learners' behaviors at all times. He describes teachers who exhibit withitness as being "tuned in" to their students' needs. They may seem to have eyes in the back of their heads and know what each student is doing, thinking, or feeling. These teachers display an ability to pick up immediately on problem behaviors and stop them before they escalate. These special educators appear to have a natural intuition that patiently advises and guides students with general expertise and wisdom.

Merriam-Webster's Collegiate Dictionary (2003, p. 1439) defines *with-it* as "socially or culturally up-to-date." Students perceive with-it teachers as keeping current with the latest trends and fads. These teachers stay abreast of the students' hobbies, interests, and other free-time activities. This awareness can be used as a bonding technique. Give assessment tools and activities titles with words, phrases, or names from students' favorite songs, movies, sitcoms, musical groups, sports, or fashion styles. Students recognize and respond to teachers who exhibit withitness because it validates the youth culture when information is bridged to their lives.

Teachers need to become so familiar with a student's hobbies and interests that it is easy to refer to these outside activities in informal conversations when an opportunity presents itself. Provide an area for students to spotlight their interests and accomplishments with photos, notes, or newspaper clippings. Knowledge of the student's personal, free-time activities and interests often provides valuable data that creates avenues for motivation, instruction, and assessment.

Table 2.3   Student-to-Student Behavior Expectations

Unacceptable Behaviors	*Valued Behaviors*
Put-Downs/Sarcasm • Is that the best you can do? • That doesn't make sense. • You didn't think through that answer.	**Encouraging Comments** • Way to go! • Good try! • Good thinking.
Negative Gestures • Frowning • Gasping in awe • Dropping the shoulders • Slumping in disappointment	**Positive Gestures** • Smiles • Thumbs-up • Nods of the head • High fives

Student-to-Student Behavior Expectations

Students need to know that unacceptable behaviors toward each other are not tolerated during assessments. Adapt Table 2.3 to your group of students. Encourage students to add ideas to the chart. Lead students through skits that demonstrate unacceptable behaviors and follow up with scenarios that illustrate valued behaviors. Culminate the activities with in-depth discussions of the behavior expectations.

Reinforce expectations whenever the opportunity arises. Use specific feedback, as in the following examples:

You made a mistake by _____, so you need to _____.

I like the way you _____. This time add _____.

Celebrate Assessment Success

Create an exciting atmosphere to celebrate learning by planning special events related to assessment. For example, choose a unique, enticing name to build anticipation and curiosity for the assessment activity day. When an assessment day is announced, use a catchy title for the day. Students are more likely to remember the assessment if they hear the teacher say,

Don't forget, on Marvelous Monday we will show what we know about _____ in our Squaring Off activity.

Examples: Days of the Week

Marvelous Monday:	Squaring Off
Terrific Tuesday:	Partner Pairing
Wacky Wednesday:	Standards, Stations, and Centers of Choice
Thinking Thursday:	Brainy Text Talk
Fantastic Friday:	Presentations and Celebrations

Promote Positive Feelings for Assessment

Find ways to generate anticipation and excitement before, during, and after assessment activities. Give learners opportunities to make suggestions and plan celebrations as in the following examples:

- Give each other a high five and a good-luck wish!
- Share a pat on the back.
- Make banners, posters, or balloons from brightly colored paper.
- Post messages that promote success, such as "Soar With Success," "Fly High!" or "Give It Your Best!"

Design each assessment strategy to entice learners to give their best efforts. Provide opportunities for students to review their results. This encourages students to keep making attempts as they see progress and growth. Select strategies that motivate students as they engage in assessment activities. Remember, motivated learners use their best efforts and thinking skills.

When someone is taught the joy of learning, it becomes a life-long process that never stops, a process that creates a logical individual.
That is the challenge and joy of teaching.

—Marva Collins

A productive climate has a significant effect on students' attitudes toward immediate and future experiences related to assessment. In this environment students realize that everyone has areas in which to improve. They learn the value of using effective strategies to identify their needs so they can become comfortable saying to themselves and others, "I don't understand this part." This statement indicates that the students are striving to "zap the gaps." When a positive learning climate is established, individuals learn to automatically assess and monitor their skills and seek assistance because they have the desire to improve. This environment empowers learners and develops their personal navigation systems for success.

Knowing **3** the Learner

The potential of a child is the most intriguing and stimulating thing in all creation.

—Ray L. Wilbur

Essential Question: How does knowledge of the learner's learning styles, intelligences, personalities, knowledge base, and interests assist in the selection and use of differentiated assessment strategies?

Effective teachers know it is worth their time to gather as much information as they can about each student and not to assume anything. This chapter provides useful strategies and ideas for gathering valuable data on each learner. It provides tips to gather information through formal and informal assessment tools. With the results, teachers can diagnose problems or situations to strategically plan for the diverse needs of individual learners.

INFORMATION GATHERING

Teachers gain knowledge of each student by noting correct, incorrect, appropriate, or inappropriate responses. It is important to have an expanded collection of tools to obtain data related to the student's level of understanding, interests, method of tackling specific problems, and individual learning style.

It takes time to think, assess, and analyze gathered information. Step back, interpret, and make the right instructional decisions. Be careful not to jump to the wrong conclusion by making incorrect assumptions and

Figure 3.1 Assessment Guides Planning

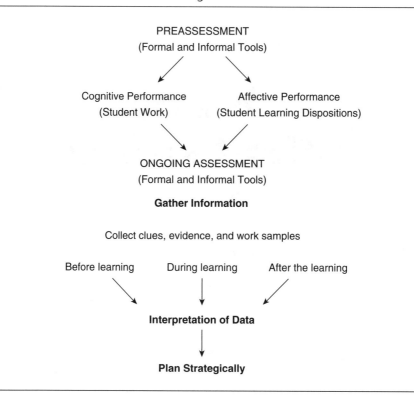

generalizations or by taking action too quickly. When a student performs below his or her potential, the alert teacher recognizes *when* this is happening, informs the student of his or her performance level, and analyzes *why* it is occurring. Adjustments are made to the plans to meet the learner's performance level.

The goal in education is for all students to learn as much as they can to be productive citizens and maintain personal success in today's world. As educators, we know all students can learn. We also know that most students can learn more than they are learning. Think about how they may be captivated for hours by a video game. This occurs because the activity is stimulating, engaging, and challenging for their minds. The bottom line is that people learn about things and techniques that interest them. Meaningful knowledge and experiences are usually stored in long-term memory. After each learning experience ask yourself, "Was the activity mentally engaging for the individual learners? Did they truly learn this information?"

A student is more likely to learn information and be able to apply it when the assessment experience comprises the following:

- Creates interest for the student
- Meets the individual's needs

- Takes place in the window of opportunity for learning
- Occurs within an appropriate time frame
- Serves a significant or practical purpose
- Is viewed as a valuable use of time
- Intrigues the student enough for him or her to invest time and energy
- Maintains commitment to the task
- Stimulates the desire to improve skills or to know more

Observing the Learner

Teachers can become practiced at considering the following questions as they observe students:

A. What is the individual's knowledge base at the beginning of the unit of study?
  1. What does the learner know?
  2. What is the student's attitude toward the new learning?
  3. How can the student's prior knowledge be assessed?

B. What does the student need to learn next?
  1. Identify the gaps in the student's learning.
  2. Analyze and prioritize needs.

C. What are the observable behaviors?
  1. Is the behavior causing a problem with the learning?
  2. How can the behavior be corrected?
  3. How will the behavior be modified?

D. How will I teach the information?
  1. What are the appropriate actions to "zap the gaps"?

E. How will I check for understanding?
  1. What assessment tools do I need to use with this learner?

F. How will the new information be retained, or "crystallized"?

GARDNER'S MULTIPLE INTELLIGENCE THEORY

In the book *If the Shoe Fits . . . : How to Develop Multiple Intelligences in the Classroom* (Chapman, 1993), the author presents Howard Gardner's eight "intelligences," or abilities, that are possessed by every individual. Students perform best when they use their strongest intelligences. Throughout life, as individuals explore and accumulate knowledge, their intelligences strengthen and grow. They can also strengthen their weaker intelligences. Sharing this theory with students gives them new ways to view their current strengths and ways to identify areas for growth.

The eight intelligences listed in Table 3.1 include the signs or names individuals might wear if they are strong in a particular intelligence. The chart also lists assessment tools and career choices that fit the intelligences. It is important to differentiate assessment experiences by choosing assessment tools that incorporate varied intelligences. This allows students to show their learning in ways that feel natural and comfortable to them.

Key Elements of Gardner's Multiple Intelligence Theory

A teacher can use the following key points to implement the multiple intelligence theory in differentiated assessment experiences:

> *It is not "how" smart you are, but how you are smart.*
>
> —Howard Gardner

Everyone is born with a genetically formed brain that is unique.

Knowledge and experiences mold and change the brain.

Everyone has at least eight intelligences.

People have three or four areas of strength among their intelligences.

Weaker intelligences can be strengthened. People learn and remember more information when participating in activities that engage their strongest intelligences.

Activity: Tear Into Your Intelligences

The following activity gives teachers and students an opportunity to conduct a self-assessment of their intelligences. It identifies three or four of an individual's strongest intelligences and at least one or two intelligences that may need to be strengthened.

1. Choose eight distinctly different colors of construction paper.

2. List the eight intelligences on a chart. Color-code the intelligences by placing a small piece of the colored construction paper beside each one. Examples: Verbal/Linguistic = orange; Naturalist = green.

3. Cut the construction paper into equal strips so everyone has one strip to match each intelligence color.

4. Label the top of each strip with the intelligence that matches the color on the chart.

Table 3.1   Meet the Intelligences

Intelligence	My Sign	Assessments Tool	Career Choices
Verbal/Linguistic	The Communicating You!	Listening Reading Writing Linking Speaking	Journalist Teacher Announcer Actor Storyteller Comedian Speaker Author
Musical/Rhythmic	The Listening You! The Musical You! The Rhythmic You!	Rhythms Beats Poems Inflections Tonal patterns	Musician Dancer Sound technician Composer Band director Poet
Logical/ Mathematical	The Gadget You! The Problem-Solving You! The Analyzing You!	Numbers Problem solving Logical thinking Puzzles Games	Inventor Programmer Analyst Technician Accountant

Visual/Spatial	The Creative You!
	The Artistic You!
	The Designer You!
		Art media
		Visualization
		Brainstorming
		Color
		   coordination
			Artist
			Designer
			Builder
			Fashion
			   coordinator
			Makeup artist
			Architect

Bodily/Kinesthetic	The Athlete You! The Tactile You!	Manipulatives Experiments Simulations Role-plays Paper folding	Actor Athlete Seamstress Lab technician Surgeon Dentist
Naturalist	The Scientific You! The Survivor You!	Working with nature Ability to survive	Environmentalist Farmer Oceanographer Astronaut Zoologist
Intrapersonal	The Goal-Setting You! The Metacognitive You!	Knowing self Accepting self Working alone	Computer program analyst Accountant
Interpersonal	The Social Butterfly You! The Team Player You!	Cooperative learning Socializing Sharing	Teacher Receptionist Talk show host

Use a key similar to the following to abbreviate the title of each intelligence:

Verbal/Linguistic = V/L   Musical/Rhythmic = M/R
Logical/Mathematical = L/M   Visual/Spatial = V/S
Bodily/Kinesthetic = B/K   Naturalist = N
Intrapersonal = Intra   Interpersonal = Inter

5. Instruct students to keep the full length of each intelligence strip that matches their three or four strongest intelligences.

6. Show them how to tear off the bottom of each intelligence strip to match their weaker intelligences. For example, the corresponding strip will be very short if the student perceives the intelligence as being extremely weak.

7. Tear off the bottom of the remaining strips so the length represents the strength or weakness of each intelligence area.

Teacher Reflection Sample

How do your strongest intelligences impact the learner and your choice of assessment tools?

Figure 3.2   Activity: Intelligences and You

Place a star beside three or four of your strongest intelligences and a check mark beside two or three of your weakest intelligences:

____ Verbal/Linguistic	____ Visual/Spatial	
____ Musical/Rhythmic	____ Naturalist	
____ Logical/Mathematical	____ Intrapersonal	
____ Bodily/Kinesthetic	____ Interpersonal	

My two or three strongest intelligences are _____, _____, and _____.

How do I learn best?
How do I like to show what I know?
The intelligences that I need to strengthen are . . . .
How do the results of the activity reflect the way you teach?

Repertoire of Assessment Tools

Teachers often plan instructional activities and assessments in their own areas of strength. For example, teachers with strong visual/spatial intelligence tend to employ art and design techniques in lessons. An individual's areas of strength may not match the teacher's area of strength. For example, struggling math students may have strengths in the area of music. They are able to learn math facts using raps, jingles, and rhymes. If teachers are not musically inclined, they must leave their comfort zones and find musical approaches to reach these musical learners. The students' favorite ways to learn are avenues to optimal results in assessment. We strongly recommend that teachers create a collection or list of assessment tools correlated with all intelligences so they will be ready to select and implement them as needed.

Research shows a number of ways to view students' intelligences, thinking, and learning styles. Analyze the complete profile of a student and its effect on how he or she approaches, engages, and demonstrates learning. Remember, use this information to provide lessons and assessments that allow each student to achieve success.

GREGORC'S THINKING STYLES

One model of individual learning styles comes from the research of Anthony F. Gregorc (1982). The Gregorc model provides an organized way to consider how the mind works. It can determine students' natural learning strengths. The theory is based on two perceptual qualities: concrete and abstract. Perceptions shape what we think, how we make decisions, and how we define what's important. Gregorc's model also includes two ordering abilities: sequential and random. All people have both concrete and abstract perceptual abilities and, to some extent, both sequential and random ordering abilities. Yet each person is usually comfortable using one more than the other.

Four combinations of the strongest perceptual and ordering abilities in each individual exist in Gregorc's model:

Concrete/random   Abstract/random
Concrete/sequential   Abstract/sequential

Each person has a unique combination of natural strengths and abilities. By learning some of the common characteristics of each of the four combinations described by Gregorc, teachers can recognize and value what students do best and help them to improve in areas that are least used and understood (Gregorc, 1979, 1982).

Table 3.2   Assessment Choices Using the Multiple Intelligences

The following list of activities and tools can be used to create a repertoire of assessment strategies. Add to the list and tailor it to your learners' needs.

Intelligence	Assessment Activities and Tools
Verbal/Linguistic	Essays Audio recordings Reports Speeches Debates Interviews Research projects Quizzes or tests Logs; journals; diaries Questions and answers Observations/findings Oral reports Explanations Written assignments Jokes Exhibits Posters Critical factual writing Creative writing Writing or telling Various genres
Musical/Rhythmic	Musical patterns Songs Raps Poetry Rhythmic patterns and beats Jingles and cheers Background sounds and noises Musical compositions Recordings
Logical/Mathematical	Sequential steps Fact analysis Research Logic problems Attribute groupings Problem-solving techniques Outlines Reasons and rationales Predictions Rubrics Demonstrations Calculations Statistics/data

Intelligence	Assessment Activities and Tools
	Research projects Graphic organizers Labels Categorizing activities Manipulatives Gadgets/calculators Formulas Thinking games Patterns Process explanations Timelines
Visual/Spatial	Color, lines, and shapes Creative designs Sculptures Visualizations Imagination Graphic organizers Visuals Art media Displays Posters Charts Brochures Pictures Illustrations Cartoons and caricatures
Bodily/Kinesthetic	Manipulatives Mimes Inventions Sports participation Demonstrations using physical movement Exercises Human representations Hands-on experiences Simulations Role-playing Field trips Demonstrations Dramatic interpretations Movement routines
Naturalist	Demonstrations of environmental sensitivity Awareness of surroundings Appreciation of nature Recognitions of science and nature Classifications Survival skills Creations of environmental scenes

(Continued)

Table 3.2 (Continued)

Intelligence	Assessment Activities and Tools
	Nature collections Problem solving in environmental situations Research of nature topics Real-life situations
Intrapersonal	Private conferences Knowledge and understanding of self Introspective diary entries Surveys Inventories Thinking Journal entries Logs Diaries Tests/exams Self-studies Contracts Personal choices Metacognitive engagement Independent work Portfolios Personal reflections
Interpersonal	Communications with others Teamwork Questions Demonstrations of intuitiveness Partner reports Reenactments Cooperative learning Text talk Participation in literary circles Human graphs Cooperative jigsaws

KOLB'S LEARNING STYLES MODEL

Developed in 1984, Kolb's learning styles model is based on whether a student prefers to process information by thinking or feeling and whether a student prefers to process information by doing or watching. Four learning style preferences emerge: activist, reflector, pragmatist, and theorist. This learning styles model is designed to be used as a guide, not as an absolute set of rules. Kolb's learning styles model can lead teachers to recognize and utilize a student's preferred learning method as the basic approach for instruction.

Learning Style	Descriptors
Accommodators	Exhibit independent, creative and flexible thinking. Risk taking leads to unique approaches to problems.
Convergers	Combine the most vital information from the facts and ideas to develop conclusions.
Assimilators	Want to know more. Enjoy working with concepts, theories, and ideas.
Divergers	Use available information to create new ideas or a variety of approaches to problems.

Table 3.3 further explores the theories of Gardner, Gregorc, and Kolb.

Profiles to Guide Student Success

In Chapter 2 we examined the domain that Goleman describes for emotional intelligence. In addition, the educator, psychologist, and author

Table 3.3   Applying the Experts' Views of Learners

Gardner's Multiple Intelligences	Gregorc's Thinking Styles	Kolb's Learning Style Profile
Language-related Verbal/Linguistic Musical/Rhythmic **Object-related** Logical/Mathematical Visual/Spatial Bodily/Kinesthetic Naturalist **Person-related** Intrapersonal Interpersonal	**Concrete Random** Experimenters Practical creators Find alternative ways **Concrete Sequential** Use details Structure their work Organizers **Abstract Sequential** Investigators Analyzers Abstract thinkers **Abstract Random** Share ideas Connect with emotions Use self-reflection	**Accommodator** Creative Flexible riskers **Convergers** Practical Organize Use essential information **Assimilators** Dig into information Abstract thinkers Want to know more **Divergers** Learn from others Look for different ways

Table 3.4 More Experts' Views

Goleman's Emotional Intelligences	*Sternberg's Triarchical Theory*

Self-Awareness
Understand feelings
Self-confidence
 	
Self-Regulation
Maintains focus
Delays gratification
Demonstrates independence
Completes tasks
 	
Motivation
Has initiative
Has the desire to learn and improve
Exhibits resilience
 	
Empathy
Feels what others are feeling
Understands the views of others
Gives support to others
 	
Social Skills
Cooperates with others
Is good team member
Works well with others to reach
   common goals
	Practical
	Gives the meaning
	Determines the usefulness
	Uses an experience in a personal way
	
	Analytical
	Digs for details
	Gives specific details, attributes, reasons,
	   and characteristics
	Researches and solves
	Breaks it into smaller steps or parts for
	   understanding
	
	Creative
	Designs a "new way"
	Uses innovative thinking and approaches
	Brainstorms many solutions

of the triarchic theory of "successful intelligence," Robert Sternberg, identifies the cognitive partnership of creativity, analysis, and practicality as the profile needed for success. Teachers can introduce these attributes and give students guidance in developing them to foster metacognitive skills. Table 3.4 presents these two views.

More Ways to View Learners

The following chart investigates various aspects of the learner to enhance differentiated instruction and assessment. Teachers usually find it easy to discuss a student's personality and emotions, but they seldom use his or her personality factors and emotional intelligences to customize learning strategies and activities. The two views on the chart True Colors Through Objects and Through Animals' Eyes are designed to engage students in analyzing the way they learn (see Table 3.5).

Table 3.5   True Colors and Through Animals' Eyes

True Colors Through Objects	Through Animals' Eyes (Chapman and King)
Color: Green—The Organizer **Object: Palm Pilot** **Traits:** 　Organized 　Needs structure 　List maker 　Thinks sequentially **Color: Gold—The Researcher** **Object: Magnifying Glass** **Traits:** 　Analyzer 　Data seeker 　Brainstormer 　Detail thinker **Color: Blue—The Friend** **Object: Teddy Bear** **Traits:** 　Needs a safe environment 　Respects others 　Team player 　Social **Color: Orange—The Adventurer** **Object: Spinning Top** **Traits:** 　Flexible 　Enjoys multitasking 　Spontaneous 　Needs choices	**Chameleon** Conforms Blends with the environment **Turtle** Methodical Slow in taking risks Takes cautious steps to reach a goal **Tiger** Plans ahead Leaps with focus **Owl** Thinker Looks for details **Parrot** Follower Needs role models **Beaver** Busy Stays on-task Structures work **Butterfly** Active Unpredictable Productive **Dog** Loyal empathizer Seeks attention Needs feedback and praise **Bat** Exhibits unconventional academic and 　personal habits Has a unique view

THROUGH ANIMALS' EYES

Use animal characteristics to assist in identifying the way an individual student approaches and works on tasks, such as a problem to solve or an assessment piece. Think about the best learning situations and strategies for students who exhibit the following characteristics:

Chameleon

The chameleon conforms to the group. As a follower, he or she is easily influenced by others. The chameleon wants to please. He or she blends in with his or her surroundings.

Turtle

The turtle thinks before making decisions. The turtle is cautious and works slowly through a process or problem. He or she maintains focus and reaches set destinations at his or her own pace.

Tiger

The tiger is a stalker. The tiger plans ahead by strategically lining up his or her attack technique. The tiger then leaps with determined fast-paced actions to get what he or she wants or to accomplish the task.

Owl

The owl is a metacognitive, wise thinker. The owl uses his or her unique vision to look at problems from various angles. This wise creature analyzes information and thinks through each step and procedure.

Parrot

The parrot mimics voices, sounds, and behaviors. His or her actions are usually dependent on interactions.

Beaver

The beaver is a hard-working team member and gets the job done. This worker eagerly approaches complex tasks, is resourceful, and works strategically. The beaver perceives his or her role as a personal mission to accomplish tasks.

Butterfly

The butterfly evolves through each step and procedure cautiously. The butterfly strives for perfection while progressing through sequential, developmental stages. He or she is very predictable and celebrates success.

Dog

The dog exhibits emotions, intuition, and feelings. The dog is aware of the feelings of others and empathizes with them. The dog strives to please. He enjoys feedback and praise.

Bat

The bat does not conform. He or she approaches tasks with a unique view. Although the bat's approaches to tasks are unconventional, this nocturnal animal accomplishes the goals.

Using DeBono's Hats to Assess Thinking

Edward DeBono (1985), an expert in creative thinking, presents his theory of Five Hats for creative thinking. These five hats provide a way to solve problems from different angles and discover alternative solutions to problems. Teachers can model the use of each hat for students to learn how to think clearly and objectively. This encourages students to be more focused, to generate ideas, to spot opportunities, and to look at problems, decisions, and opportunities systematically. This gives students a better understanding of their own thinking as well as the thinking of others.

White Hat

Needs and gathers the information

Purple Hat

Is cautious. Sees the flip side

Yellow Hat

Has an optimistic view. Looks at the benefits, positive aspects

Green Hat

Brainstorms new ideas, ways, or possibilities

Blue Hat

Reflects and practices metacognition

Challenge students to design a chart that reflects their learning styles and characteristics. Provide examples of various descriptors and indicators. Ask them to replace the hat descriptors by choosing a general category and indicators from games, shoes, musical instruments, or sports. This activity engages the learners in constructing a self-assessment tool.

Assess On-Task Behaviors

Anxiety and stress may block or interrupt concentration so deeply that students exhibit dependent behaviors while working on assigned tasks. If learners have adequate background knowledge and experience, they are more likely to exhibit independence. Students who become self-regulated and self-directed in their approaches to assessment tasks are more likely to demonstrate initiative and responsibility as learners (see Tables 3.6, 3.7, and 3.8 and Figure 3.3).

Table 3.6   Dependent and Independent Behaviors

Use the following chart to become acquainted with the students' characteristics as dependent and independent learners. Use the information to develop the behaviors they need for success in academic and personal activities.

Dependent Behaviors	Independent Behaviors
• Has little or no prior experience • Lacks strategies and skills • Has difficulty comprehending oral or written directions • Exhibits little or no persistence • Does not try when tasks become difficult • Lacks memory skills to retain and recall directions, skills, formulas, and rules • Depends on others for assistance and guidance	• Monitors own learning • Paces work based on difficulty and time allotment • Uses self-reflection to identify needs • Knows and applies various strategies • Requests assistance as a last resort • Applies memory strategies • Works without assistance

Figure 3.3   Activity: Getting to Know ME: An Object View. Give students the following activity as a way for them to explore understanding of themselves as learners.

1. Number the four objects in the order that they symbolize you.

   a. ____ Palm Pilot b. ____ Magnifying Glass c. ____ Teddy Bear d. ____ Spinning Top

2. List the objects in the order that they symbolize you and complete each sentence.

   a. I am *most* like a _____ because I _____.

   b. I am also like a _____ because I _____.

   c. I am also like a _____ because I _____.

   d. I am *least* like a _____ because I _____.

Table 3.7   An Object View of Learners

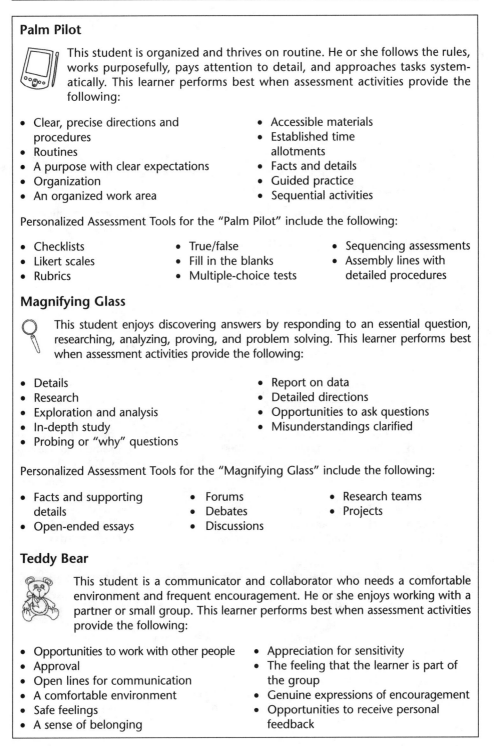

Palm Pilot

This student is organized and thrives on routine. He or she follows the rules, works purposefully, pays attention to detail, and approaches tasks systematically. This learner performs best when assessment activities provide the following:

- Clear, precise directions and procedures
- Routines
- A purpose with clear expectations
- Organization
- An organized work area

- Accessible materials
- Established time allotments
- Facts and details
- Guided practice
- Sequential activities

Personalized Assessment Tools for the "Palm Pilot" include the following:

- Checklists
- Likert scales
- Rubrics

- True/false
- Fill in the blanks
- Multiple-choice tests

- Sequencing assessments
- Assembly lines with detailed procedures

Magnifying Glass

This student enjoys discovering answers by responding to an essential question, researching, analyzing, proving, and problem solving. This learner performs best when assessment activities provide the following:

- Details
- Research
- Exploration and analysis
- In-depth study
- Probing or "why" questions

- Report on data
- Detailed directions
- Opportunities to ask questions
- Misunderstandings clarified

Personalized Assessment Tools for the "Magnifying Glass" include the following:

- Facts and supporting details
- Open-ended essays

- Forums
- Debates
- Discussions

- Research teams
- Projects

Teddy Bear

This student is a communicator and collaborator who needs a comfortable environment and frequent encouragement. He or she enjoys working with a partner or small group. This learner performs best when assessment activities provide the following:

- Opportunities to work with other people
- Approval
- Open lines for communication
- A comfortable environment
- Safe feelings
- A sense of belonging

- Appreciation for sensitivity
- The feeling that the learner is part of the group
- Genuine expressions of encouragement
- Opportunities to receive personal feedback

(Continued)

Table 3.7 (Continued)

Personalized Assessment Tools for the "Teddy Bear" include the following:

- Inventories
- Surveys
- Partner and small group learning

- Conferences
- Personal feedback
- Cooperative tasks

Spinning Top

This student enjoys a variety of creative choices. He or she thrives on fast-paced, hands-on challenges. The Spinning Top is an eager, active participant who enjoys creating projects or games. This learner performs best when assessment activities provide the following:

- Choices
- Variety
- Creativity
- Practical applications

- Fun, stimulating activities
- Hands-on, multitask activities

- Fast-paced, exciting challenges
- Celebrations

Personalized Assessment Tools for the "Spinning Top" include the following:

- Demonstrations
- Simulations

- Experiments
- Projects

- Choice boards
- Role-playing

Table 3.8   Four Ways of Knowing and Showing

Yet another perspective on how students differ in the ways they prefer to show learning comes from the work of Carl Jung and Isabel Briggs Myers. The following chart is adapted from the work of Silver, Strong, and Perini (2000). Use the ideas as examples of ways to assess the students in the ways they prefer to demonstrate their knowledge.

Self-Expressive	Mastery	Understanding	Interpersonal
Needs to explain in his or her own way	Needs to report, memorize, practice, and exhibit	In-depth understanding	Feelings and attitudes emphasized
Assessment Tasks	**Assessment Tasks**	**Assessment Tasks**	**Assessments Tasks**
Interpret Create Design Act out Demonstrate Draw	Report it Practice and demonstrate Reach a goal or standard Complete a deductive task Respond to short-answer tests Show it	Compare and contrast Explore Use an inquiry model Make discoveries Use facts to form opinions Solve *why* and *how* Research Analyze Critique	Give points of view Relate personally Simulate actions and events Engage in cooperative events Engage in team competitions Participate in celebrations

SOURCE: Adapted from Silver, Strong, and Perini (2000).

Provide Time for Journaling

Assign journal writing in various formats so students can openly share what they know—their thoughts, questions, and concerns before, during, and after learning. Avoid repeating the same journal entry formats and genres. Present a variety of ways for students to show their thinking processes, attitudes, learning, and needs in novel, intriguing ways.

Listen, Talk, Learn, and Know

Engage students in productive conversations. Listen and find out what students know and what makes them do the things they do. Sometimes these conversations are about their personal lives as well as school matters. Ask for suggestions and be open to responses. Be aware that some comments are private, and others are open to discussion. Be sensitive to the appropriate times for each type of discussion.

Work Preference Surveys

Survey students to identify their work preferences. Guide learners to understand that they often play a role in the way they set up the classroom environment for assessments. Students do the best work when their preferences are accommodated. The teacher can analyze the results and discover how to assess the learners.

The following instrument is designed to discover each learner's favorite ways to work. Use the results to accommodate the student's working preferences whenever it is practical and appropriate during instruction or assessment experiences.

LEARN TO BE AN OBSERVER

Digging Deep Into Assessment

Break an observation into manageable parts by looking at the different levels of a student's performance related to a standard. Use a scale to analyze the student's knowledge and ability level. This differentiated assessment view reflects the student's breadth and depth of understanding.

As an example, the scale in Figure 3.5 on page 47 presents one way to dig deeper into the student's vocabulary level in a content area. Use the identified level as the entry point to teach vocabulary skills.

After the student's performance level is identified in relation to a grade-level standard, use the assessment data to plan and begin the next step of instruction at the student's readiness level.

Figure 3.4   Work Preference Survey

Name _____   Date _____

1. I prefer to work with

    _____ because _____.

    _____ because _____.

    _____ because _____.

2. I do not like to work with

    _____ because _____.

    _____ because _____.

    _____ because _____.

3. I would rather work

    _____ alone _____ with a partner _____ with a small group

    Why? _____

4. My favorite type of assignment in a group is _____ because _____.

5. My favorite type of assignment with a partner is _____ because _____.

6. My favorite type of assignment to complete alone is _____ because _____.

7. The best thing about group work is _____.

8. The worst thing about group work is _____.

Other comments are _____.

While Observing and Assessing

Ask yourself, "Can the student communicate his or her thinking?"

Notice the student who simply solves problems without details, inside thinking, sequential steps, or other thinking processes.

Figure 3.5   Looking at Performance From Lowest to Highest

Lowest Performing Level

1. The teacher shows several pictures and says, "Find the picture of the _____."
The student points to the picture.

2. The teacher shows a picture, and the student identifies it orally.

3. The teacher shows a picture. The student identifies the picture and gives details about it from his or her background and experiences.

4. The teacher provides the picture. The student matches the picture to the written identification label.

5. The teacher provides the word. The student draws a matching picture.

6. The teacher provides the picture. The student writes the word.

7. The teacher orally presents the word. The student writes, illustrates, and explains the term.

Highest Performing Level

Be aware of the point or place where the student begins to falter or fail to complete the task.

Listen carefully for the student who views information from a different angle, approaches a problem in an innovative way, uses a unique process, generates new ideas, or creates an alternate but acceptable solution.

Observation Tips

Ask yourself the following:

Is the student capable of communicating his or her thinking?

Is the student rushing carelessly through the steps?

Did the student correctly verbalize inside thinking to process the steps or procedures?

SHOW STUDENTS HOW TO KNOW THEMSELVES AND EACH OTHER

Explicitly teach students how to reflect on their own likes and dislikes related to their interests, their personality traits, and the many ways they learn. Remind students that this information is not to be used as a way to apply personal labels. Discuss with the class the many ways their abilities, knowledge, and interests change through experiences.

Use activities similar to the following to give students various ways to get to know themselves and each other. They can use this knowledge during activities such as self-reflections or self-talk to improve their assessment performances.

Sharing Personal Information

Develop personal bonds with students. It is easier to become acquainted with students' interests and hobbies if they feel comfortable. The following activity gives individual students an opportunity to share personal information. Use the summary sentences as basic assessment data.

Activity: Conceal and Reveal

1. Tell each student to bring three objects that symbolize him or her to class.
   a. Use the following as examples:
      i. If you enjoy music, choose a CD.
      ii. If you enjoy gardening, bring in some seeds.
      iii. If you like to travel, choose a map.

2. Conceal the objects in a box, sack, or other container so they remain hidden until it is time to reveal each one.

3. Find a space for pairs of students to work together.

4. Tell students to face each other and name themselves Partner A and Partner B.
   a. Partner A takes out his first concealed object and uses it to tell something about himself.
   b. Partner B then takes out his first concealed object and uses it to tell something about himself.
   c. Continue sharing all the objects to find out as much as you can about each other from the discussion of each item.

5. Give partners time to introduce each other to the class by sharing facts or interesting comments related to the objects.

6. Examples: Bill likes to _____. Rosa takes _____ lessons.

Ask students to write one sentence about their partners using each object. Collect the sentences to create a data record of the information gathered during the activity.

Figure 3.6   **Activity:** *I'm All That* Hat. This activity is designed to identify the student's confidence level, interests, intelligences, learning preferences, and communication skills.

I'm All That Hat: Directions

1. Draw a hat in the center of a piece of paper.

2. Use directions similar to the following as a self-survey:

   a. Write your name in a decorative way on the front and center portion of the hat.

   b. Think of a "famous title" that describes you, and write it under your name. Examples: Mechanical Wizard   Soccer Star   Game Guru   Math Master

   c. On the right side of the hat, draw or write the thing(s) you do best.

   d. On the left side of the hat, draw or write the way you learn best.

   e. Write the best thing(s) about you as a student across the top of the hat.

   f. Add symbols, decorations, and details in the spaces on the hat to show important things about you.

   g. Share the information on your hat with a partner.

   h. End the presentation saying, "Yes, I'm all that . . . and *more.*"

Activity: Put Up and Pass

This activity develops self-esteem and builds confidence. Each individual receives a "Put-Up," or sincere praise statement from all team members. Explain to students that these are the opposites of put-downs. These positive statements lead to success during assessment experiences.

Follow the directions to prepare for the team "Put-Ups." Students will need their *I'm All That* Hats for the last portion of this activity.

Activity: My Silhouette Featurette

The Silhouette Featurette activity is a novel way to gather valuable information about each learner. This is a unique strategy to use as an introduction to graphic organizers. Teachers should participate in this activity, if possible, so students can get to know their special interests, skills, and hobbies.

Note: The Silhouette Featurette is used in the following activity.

Figure 3.7 Put Up and Pass

Put Up and Pass Directions

Write the name of each person on your team on a sheet of paper.

Choose one adjective to make each person feel like a special, valued team member. Write the "Put-up" word that describes each person beside his or her name. Hide the paper so no one can see it.

Choose a team member to be the Put-up receiver for the first round. Each individual takes a turn sharing the adjective with the receiver. In one sentence he or she tells why the adjective fits the receiver.

Examples: *friendly*—You always want to share.

creative—You have neat ideas.

The receiving member of the Put-up adjectives writes the word near or around his or her *I'm All That* Hat. The only words the receiver can say are *Thank you!*

Continue until each individual receives a Put-up from each team member.

Put up the Put-ups for all to see!

Activity: Shadow Show

The Shadow Show gives students a chance to become familiar with their classmates. Again, the teacher's participation adds to the anticipation and excitement. Instruct the students to tape the Silhouette Featurette on their clothing so the head of the silhouette appears directly below their necks. Ask everyone to wear his or her silhouette and form a circle.

Shadow Show Directions

The teacher begins the Shadow Show by introducing himself or herself and modeling the procedure. The personal descriptive information on his own T-shirt is shared with the group. He ends his presentation and introduces the first student on his left using the student's "Famous Title" and saying, "I would like to introduce Jim, the Drawing Dynamo!" Discuss the diversity and uniqueness of individuals exhibited through the introductions.

Figure 3.8   My Silhouette Featurette

My Silhouette Featurette Instructions

1. Fold a large sheet of chart paper in half using a lengthwise, or "hot dog," fold.

2. Begin on the fold and draw an outline of one side of your body as it appears in a silhouette. (Notes: If needed, show an example of a silhouette. Ask a volunteer to stand between the light of a projector and a screen. Cover half of the projected silhouette with a large sheet of paper.)

3. Begin on the fold, and cut around the silhouette. (Remind students to begin cutting on the fold.)

4. Cut out your silhouette. Add hair, facial details, and other physical features that give a picture of you.

5. Dress your silhouette by drawing a T-shirt, other clothing, and accessories.

6. Use the following directions to create a self-survey with the silhouette

   a. Place your name in a decorative way in the center of your T-shirt.

   b. Write a "Famous Title" for you under your name.

   Examples:

   Drawing Dynamo   Born to Dance   The Music Man

   Computer Wizard

7. On one sleeve draw or write the thing(s) you do best.

8. On the other sleeve draw or write the way you learn best.

9. On the T-shirt, list your interests or hobbies.

   a. Add details to your Silhouette Featurette that tell important things about you.

   b. Add new items, facts, or ideas each day to the gallery picture created of you.

Review the definition and characteristics of a graphic organizer. Relate this information to the information gathered on the Shadow Show designs. Post the silhouettes to create a Silhouette Featurette Gallery. Join the class as they tour the gallery and make notes. Encourage students to add more information to their gallery picture every day.

Variation: Create a Silhouette Featurette of a factual or fictional character as an assessment activity.

Activity: Show Your True Colors

Introduce and read Dr. Seuss's book *My Many Colored Days.* Each color in the story reflects an emotion. For example, yellow is depicted as a bright, busy day, whereas purple reflects a sad day. Share the meaning of the phrase "show your true colors" to encourage students to reveal their emotions and attitudes. Once this activity is introduced, it can be used before, during, or after assessment experiences.

1. Cut a circle from construction paper to match each color and emotion described in the Dr. Seuss book.

2. Ask each student to display the colored circle that reflects his or her attitude toward a new topic before, during, or after the learning.

3. Use the colored disks as prompts with journal activities to provide opportunities for students to reflect on their attitudes associated with specific assessment or learning experiences.

ASSESSING INDEPENDENT WORK HABITS

Independent tasks provide opportunities to analyze the student's on-task behaviors, study skills, learning styles, intelligences, and level of independence. For example, one handy assessment tool is the Likert scale (see Figure 3.9). It can be easily marked during assignments and analyzed quickly when time permits. The number two is used to represent the lowest level. This avoids giving the learners zeros and ones. The numbers may be repeated as the cheer "two, four, six, eight." The number eight represents the highest level. The learner places an "X" on each scale above the number that reflects his or her work, behavior, feelings, knowledge base, or understanding. Give learners an opportunity to write or tell why "X" marks the identified spot on their scale.

Variation: The student may use the scale as a self-analysis.

Teachers can give students opportunities to use these scales for self-evaluation. Compare and discuss the learner and teacher scores.

TEACHING ASSESSMENT STRATEGIES TO STUDENTS

Introduce each new assessment strategy so everyone understands the term(s) and the process before using it. This alleviates fear of the unknown

Figure 3.9   Observation Criteria for Student Work Habits

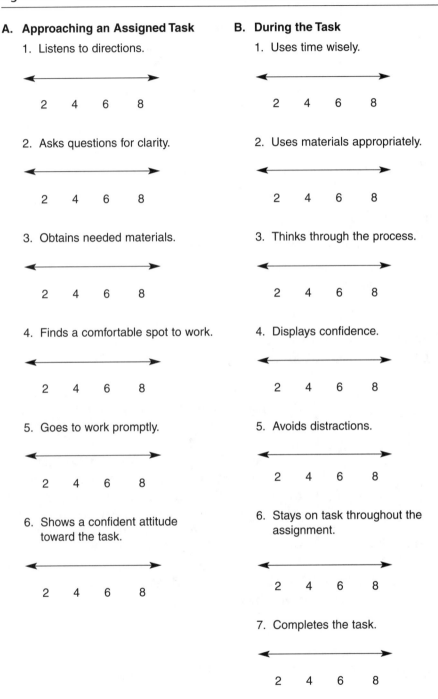

A. Approaching an Assigned Task

1. Listens to directions.

   2   4   6   8

2. Asks questions for clarity.

   2   4   6   8

3. Obtains needed materials.

   2   4   6   8

4. Finds a comfortable spot to work.

   2   4   6   8

5. Goes to work promptly.

   2   4   6   8

6. Shows a confident attitude toward the task.

   2   4   6   8

B. During the Task

1. Uses time wisely.

   2   4   6   8

2. Uses materials appropriately.

   2   4   6   8

3. Thinks through the process.

   2   4   6   8

4. Displays confidence.

   2   4   6   8

5. Avoids distractions.

   2   4   6   8

6. Stays on task throughout the assignment.

   2   4   6   8

7. Completes the task.

   2   4   6   8

and presents assessment as an integral part of learning. See the examples in the suggested guideline that follows. Each step is designed to generate thinking about the many ways to present assessment.

1. Identify the assessment strategy or tool.

2. Write the name of the assessment strategy in large colorful letters on a chart or poster. Use an appealing writing style or unusual fonts to make the visual unique.

3. Pronounce the strategy's name.

4. Ask the student to echo or repeat the pronunciation.

5. Explain the purpose of the strategy and its usefulness as a lifelong tool for learning.

6. Give examples of how this strategy will benefit the student.

7. Lead a discussion about how people apply this assessment strategy in their careers and daily living.

8. Model the steps in the strategy.

9. Teach the learner to ask the question, "How am I going to remember this assessment strategy?"

> *My heart is singing for joy this morning. A miracle has happened! The light of understanding has shone upon my little pupil's mind, and behold, all things are changed!*
>
> —Annie Sullivan

For example, follow the steps above, and demonstrate how the Think Aloud strategy is used to talk through a thinking or problem-solving process. Verbalize your inside thinking processes with each step so students can hear your thoughts as you work through the procedures. According to Davey (1983), the Think Aloud technique enhances thinking as the learner visualizes, connects ideas, monitors understanding, and finds solutions.

Lead the student through a few practice rounds using this technique. Remind the student to verbalize his or her inside thinking, or Think Aloud, with each step.

MAKE ASSESSMENT STRATEGIES PERSONALLY MEANINGFUL

Find Out All About Me

According to Mithaug, Mithaug, Martin, Martin, and Wehmeyer (2003), students need opportunities to develop personal control of their learning experiences. Their research emphasizes the importance of student choice, self-determination, self-regulation, and self-management. Learners who have these characteristics are more likely to sustain their work toward goals, adapt learned information to new situations, and become successful in their learning experiences.

Survey Learners of Other Cultures

How can assessment be designed to meet the needs of diverse learners? The Southwest Educational Development Lab (SEDL) publication *Making Assessment Work for Everyone: How to Build on Student Strengths* (Kusimo et al., 2000) offers research and information to help teachers make the assessment process equitable and beneficial for all students and teachers. Teachers can use the following outline to guide student assessment:

- Clear and appropriate learning targets

- Clearly focused and appropriate purpose for assessment

- Appropriate match among targets, purposes, and methods of assessment

- Sufficient sampling of student work to make sound inferences about learning

- Fairness and freedom from biases that distort the picture of learning (Kusimo et al., 2000)

A student's cultural background and experiences profoundly impact the way he or she responds to an assessment tool. For example, girls in Asian cultures learn to be quiet and reserved. Use the information gathered in surveys, inventories, and other assessment tools to differentiate for the students from other cultures. Gather information from parents, the second-language teacher, and the interpreter. Review the characteristics, beliefs, and traditions of the culture. Use the information to provide the student with a comfortable learning environment where diversity is respected and celebrated.

Include prompts similar to the following in an inventory or survey to gather information about a student from another culture.

The student's first language is _____.

The student attended school in _____.

The student shows that he or she understands the directions by _____.

The student is able to explain the directions by _____.

To be successful, this student needs _____.

Cultural traditions and routines that may impact student assessment are _____.

In choosing the best assessment for a student of another culture, consider his or her dominant language, social behaviors, learning styles, intelligences, and level of acculturation. Administer a survey to identify the following:

- General customs practiced in the home
- Level of confidence and security
- Learning styles

- Strengths
- Needs
- Academic level
- Interests

Assessing Students' Personal Interests

The following activities provide a view of the student's internal values. Analyze the student's hobbies and interests in informal settings. Provide activities that place the student in a relaxed atmosphere of fun that provides freedom to express his or her feelings. Use the data to personalize lessons. Remember, interest is a key motivational tool that stimulates the desire to learn and enhances memory.

Recognize diversity in students' personalities. Recent research studies emphasize the value of recognizing the individual traits of a learner. Use the information to differentiate activities. For example, if the student is very sociable, he or she works well in group activities. Provide opportunities for the student to work toward independence by providing support and encouragement as he or she works alone.

Conduct Surveys, Inventories, and Questionnaires

Use inventories, surveys, and questionnaires at the beginning of the year (Tomlinson, 1999) to get to know your students' interests, values, attitudes, emotions, and areas of strength and weakness. By getting each individual to reveal this vital information, both the student and the teacher can understand the value of each student's unique learning power.

Chapman and King add to this idea by suggesting that teachers use these instruments periodically throughout the year to maintain current knowledge of students. Each student is growing with new experiences, interests, and learning opportunities that need to be realized and expressed. Different students show their abilities and capabilities at different times. By learning as much as possible about each student throughout the school year, a teacher can differentiate assessment to meet the individual's needs.

With these tools students learn to respect individual differences in themselves and others. When this breakthrough occurs, differentiation makes sense and results in individual learning. Tailor instruction to the total student's needs: social, emotional, physical, and academic. Provide ways to engage and motivate students with productive, challenging opportunities.

Sample Survey Questions

Students answer the questions in Figure 3.10 with either a *yes* or a *no* answer. Fill in the blank or rate their feelings from *yes* to *no* on a 4–1 scale. For very young students, the survey can be given orally and answers recorded.

Figure 3.10   Student Survey

Student Survey

Name _____   **Date** _____

Answer the following questions with either a *yes* or *no* answer or fill in the blank.

	Yes			No
I like to read.	4	3	2	1
I like to make up songs.	4	3	2	1
I am challenged by things that are difficult to do.	4	3	2	1
Taking things apart and reassembling them intrigues me.	4	3	2	1
I like to play outside.	4	3	2	1
I prefer to work by myself.	4	3	2	1
I enjoy working with others.	4	3	2	1
I like to draw my own pictures.	4	3	2	1
I like school.	4	3	2	1

At school, I like _____

because _____.

I do not like _____,

because _____.

If I have free time, I prefer to _____ or _____.

My favorite thing to read is _____.

Open-Ended Survey: Postlearning

Use the following examples of open-ended statements to receive feedback after a topic of study. Use the information for planning.

- I was confused about _____.
- It was easy to _____.
- I will remember _____.
- I visualized _____.
- I need to know more about _____.
- If I had known _____, it would _____.
- I would change the directions to _____.
- I would change the assessment by _____.

KNOW THE LEARNER'S UNIQUE WAYS OF COMPREHENDING

It is important to know how students comprehend best so they have opportunities to use their favorite approach when reading assigned passages. Students often have a higher comprehension level when they use their preferred way to understand passages.

Use the following technique to assess a learner's unique reading approach to understanding. It is adapted from Chapman and King's book *Differentiated Instructional Strategies for Reading in the Content Area* (2003a). The student often knows how he or she comprehends best, so ask him or her to talk about it. Select four passages on his or her instructional level, so the material is not too frustrating or too easy. Use the following guidelines to assess the unique way the learner best comprehends passages:

1. Have the student read one passage aloud and respond to explicit questions.

2. Read the next passage to the student, and ask questions about it.

3. Ask the student to read the last passage silently and respond to questions.

4. Ask the student to choose his or her favorite way to read from the above options and ask the comprehension questions.

Observe during each activity to see if the student needs to move his or her lips; use silent hums or a low, soft voice; read silently; or have someone read to him or her. The results show the teacher and the student the way he or she comprehends material the best.

Assess Oral Reading

Check comprehension ability by asking the learner to read brief, high-interest passages. Ask the student to orally retell the events in two to three sentences. Use various levels of questions based on Bloom's Taxonomy. Begin the questions with *Who, What, When, Where, Why,* and *How.* Analyze the responses. If the reader cannot answer the questions that require simple recall of facts and basic reasoning, the material is too difficult. Repeat the assessment with a passage on a lower reading level.

Choose high-interest, brief passages to read aloud. Ask questions similar to those in the silent reading examples. The student's responses demonstrate how much he or she comprehends while listening to the reading.

Sample Oral Comprehension Check

1. When did the events in this passage occur?

2. Who were the most important characters in the passage?

3. How did the characters feel?

4. What were the important events in this passage?

5. How did the characters become involved in this situation?

6. Do you think the characters will be successful? Why or why not?

TEACHING SELF-ASSESSMENT

Self-assessment gives the learners a sense of ownership and responsibility. Pride develops as individuals see how much they have learned from the entry point through the end of the study. Involving them in the assessment process improves learning.

Strategically plan to engage students in daily assessment opportunities. When students are involved in creating and planning activities, their confidence increases. They are motivated to continue learning and to want to do more. Emphasize achievement rather than failure and defeat (Stiggins, 2001). This promotes the *I can do this!* attitude instead of *I don't get it!* Each successful step moves students from their current positions toward their learning goals. They need to ask themselves the following questions:

What do I need next to accomplish this goal or task?

What help do I need?

How can I close the gap?

The answers to self-assessment questions become guides to the next steps in learning. Pupils of all ages can learn to self-assess. The process provides opportunities for monitoring and communicating their progress.

Performance Level Titles for the Assessed Learner

Novice, apprentice, practitioner, and *expert* are terms often used in rubrics and Likert scales to identify the progress of student performance at the time of the measurement. Consider the following explanations and needs as you assist learners on each performance level.

Provide novice learners with the information they need to fill in the gaps of the background knowledge they need to learn information. Students at the other levels are able to solve the problem. They find solutions on their level of understanding, in their own way. As they learn more and gain confidence, their responses become more sophisticated. The strategies and activities are designed to fit the learner's readiness level.

As students grow in their knowledge base, they are able to adapt the information and apply it to real-life situations. This information and experience becomes a part of their memory banks. The teacher analyzes the data to see who needs to move on to a new piece of learning and who needs extended practice. Reflections are used to continually review and revise effective teaching practices.

Table 3.9   Learning Performance Levels

Level	Performance Indicators	Needs
Novice	Little or no understanding of information Limited background or foundation	Needs background to be ready for new learning
Apprentice	Demonstrates some understanding of information Has some background experience	Ready for the task
Practitioner	Shows understanding of the concepts	Needs alternative applications and practice of the task
Expert	Demonstrates a deep understanding of *what, why, how,* and can explain them Able to apply information to other situations	Needs a more challenging version of the task

Involve students as active participants in making assessment decisions. For instance, ask one of the following questions:

What parts do you know and understand?

What do you need next?

Look for opportunities to give learners ownership in decisions that affect their improvement and growth. This encourages students to practice self-reflection techniques. Let them know how their suggestions influence planning.

Assessing Previous Performance

Consider waiting until students have been in your classroom a few weeks before delving into achievement records from the previous year. This allows you to develop a picture of learners' abilities and skills without preconceived ideas. Keep in mind that a student often exhibits different attitudes and levels of effort with each teacher.

Airasian (2001) uses the term *hearsay* in reference to comments from others about a student. Individuals who make statements related to a student's background, ability, or behavior usually have good intentions. They believe the information prepares the new teacher for the student. Listen, and then carefully screen the information embedded in the statements. Keep in mind that some informal comments may provide vital data that impacts assessment performance. Think positively when you encounter negative statements containing phrases similar to the following:

When someone says . . .	Use these self-reminders . . .
He is so bad that he	A student usually behaves for me.
His entire class has always been	I develop positive reputations.
His parents won't	Parents become my partners in teaching.
You will never get him to	I'll find ways to motivate him.

Apply What You Know About Students

Be cognizant of the students' current knowledge, successes, and progress. Develop a collection of diagnostic tools to gather data related to individual students. Carefully analyze the data. Mentally prepare for a myriad of possible needs. Unexpected needs may arise, but if you are ready to assist with the most common needs and are prepared to provide immediate feedback and guidance, the students will benefit. Be thoroughly familiar with various differentiated assessment strategies and tools so you can diagnose problems, gather personal data, and promptly assist the learner.

> *Remember, the more you know about your students, the more effective you will be. (Chapman & King, 2000)*

Most assessments are designed to know students as people and learners. These results form the basis for planning. In future chapters we will examine ways to incorporate this knowledge of students into differentiated assessment.

Assessing 4 Before and During Learning

Essential Questions

- How will preassessment tools optimize planning for individual needs?
- How can various differentiated assessment tools be used for immediate intervention during learning experiences to keep students on
  track in their learning adventures?

Effective teachers use ongoing assessment by continuously monitoring
progress before, during, and after learning to guide instruction. They
recognize students' needs, provide assistance with skills, clarify directions,
and motivate. This chapter provides information with formal and informal
tools to assess students before learning. It also presents practical, take-to-
the-classroom activities for assessment during learning.

ASSESSMENT BEFORE LEARNING

Preassessment is an essential prerequisite for effective diagnosis and planning. The teacher preassesses the learner's knowledge base and experiences
in relation to the upcoming topic or skill. The information gathered establishes the starting point for planning learning experiences. When teachers
strategically administer preassessments before planning their lessons, they
can address the students' strengths and needs during instruction.

Consider the value of preassessment presented in the following
scenario. A physical education teacher is gathering information to develop

lesson plans to teach volleyball. A preassessment reveals that a few students have no knowledge or experiences in relation to the sport. Their exposure to the game needs to begin with the fundamentals. Some students know the basics of the game, the rules and regulations, and understand their role in the game. They need to engage in activities that perfect specific skills. These learners review the techniques, rules, and practice, but they do not need to learn the fundamentals of the game. The information would be boring and disengaging, and more important, their valuable time is better spent learning more complex skills. The individuals who play the game and are proficient with the skills need to participate in activities that improve their speed and accuracy. This scenario applies to most learning situations.

Strong preassessments reveal the following about the individual student:

- Knowledge base and background experience
- Interests and talents
- Attitudes, likes, and dislikes
- Feelings and emotions
- Entry point for new information

Effective preassessment tools eliminate wasted time and energy during instruction. Every teacher has the challenging and rewarding task to make each lesson meaningful for all learners.

Teachers who differentiate continuously assess students' readiness to identify the next steps in a procedure, to move to the next level, or to approach new skills or concepts. The term *readiness* means "prepared." The state of readiness, or entry point, for a new skill or concept is key to the learner's success. Teachers apply this strategy when they are thinking, "Does he know to know how to _____ before we begin _____?"

> *Teach by doing whenever you can and only fall back upon words when doing it is out of the question.*
>
> —Rousseau

Administering a variety of assessments before learning unveils the student's prior knowledge and experiences in relation to the topic or skill. The teacher analyzes the results to determine the individual's readiness level and to identify the appropriate entry point for instruction.

Observation

Teacher observation is one of the most effective assessment tools. It is important to explain the purpose and value of observations to students. When the teacher stands beside individuals while recording data, the observed students are likely to become anxious. The class needs to know that the notes are used to help them learn and improve.

Observation is a valuable assessment tool because the teacher collects data as the learner engages in an activity or assignment. With experience teachers develop keen visual, auditory, and other perceptual skills to identify a student's academic skills, strengths, needs, abilities, behaviors, social interactions, health, emotions, reactions, feelings, and attitudes. This flexible assessment tool can be used anytime, in any environment, and under any circumstance. More information about this topic is presented in the section on Anecdotal Assessment (see Chapter 5). Teachers need to observe students before and during learning to do the following:

- Document progress
- Record strengths and needs
- Select appropriate resources and materials
- Report progress to students, parents, and specialists
- Support and guide instruction
- Find patterns of behavior
- Record specific observable behavior

> *The art of teaching is the art of assisting discovery.*
>
> —Mark Van Doren

PERSONALIZE INSTRUCTIONAL PLANNING

Differentiated assessment personalizes or customizes instructional plans for individual learners. A variety of preassessment tools gather data about students so as much information as possible is available to strategically design plans. Continuously strive to create a positive learning environment that is physically, emotionally, and socially tailored to the needs of individual learners.

It is important to identify the learners' attitudes, or mind-sets, toward an upcoming topic or subject. Everyone avoids unpleasant experiences, but negativity is a formidable barrier to success. When students experience negative thoughts and attitudes, their desire to work on assigned tasks is diminished.

The familiar adage "You can lead a horse to water, but you can't make him drink" can be applied to a student's attitude. If a student has had unpleasant experiences or memories of a situation, a subject, or an activity, it is difficult to change the feelings, rebuild confidence, and create the desire to engage in an assessment task. Return to the saying about the horse. You may not be able to make him *drink*, but you can make the horse very *thirsty* if you feed him a large amount of sweet oats! In a similar way, the teacher can kindle a student's desire to work successfully on assessment activities by providing enticing, meaningful experiences.

How does a teacher discover the students' feelings and emotions as they relate to upcoming topics? The most obvious way is to ask them! Use informal and formal assessments that engage students in expressing themselves. The goal is to unleash their individual "gut reactions." Select assessment tools that identify feelings and emotions so that specific strategies address these needs.

To personalize instructional planning, it is important to know how to use a variety of differentiated assessment tools to collect information about students. Use preplanning assessment tools and activities to do the following:

- Gather information for planning
- Add novelty and build interest
- Generate anticipation and excitement for upcoming lessons
- Target the learners' unique strengths and needs

Use a preassessment preview two to three weeks before designing lesson plans for the unit. This simple, effective idea builds anticipation, generates interest, and gives students ownership in learning through the assessment experiences. Think about movie advertisements. Weeks before a movie is released, its previews are accompanied with interviews of the leading actresses and actors. Promotions appear on billboards, magazines, newspapers, television, radio, and the Internet. It is obvious that this hype is designed to build anticipation and entice patrons. By the time the movie is released, individuals are "hooked." Use this approach to generate excitement and anticipation for new skills and topics.

Use the following preassessment activities one to three weeks before a unit of study begins. Assessment-gathering techniques, as illustrated in the following examples, are essential to planning for differentiated instruction.

Ponder and Pass

Ponder and Pass is a quick, informal preassessment activity that gathers valuable information. Tell students the topic of the coming unit. Then pass a notepad around the class. Challenge students to write notes about information they know related to the topic, skills they need to learn, facts they want to learn, and questions they may have.

Examples

- My background or experience on this topic is _____.
- I want to learn _____.
- My feelings about the topic of _____ are

  _____ and _____.

Select probing questions and statements that meet your assessment needs. Encourage students to submit prompts for the Ponder and Pass activity.

Response Cards

Response cards are effective and engaging preassessment tools. They can be used to quickly and efficiently assess before, during, and after instruction. While they assist the teacher in gauging the learners' prior knowledge, interest, confidence, or anxiety on a topic, they also give students valuable practice in metacognition, or thinking about their own thinking. The cards are made with two or more possible answers. Students choose a response by pointing to their answer.

As seen in the following examples, response cards are highly adaptable instruments. The following response card samples are designed as informal preassessment activities. The cards are designed with the same response choices written in precisely the same place on the front and back of the card.

Tell students to respond by placing their thumb on the response that faces them and their pointer finger on the response facing the teacher. This makes the chosen response visible on each side of the card, so the student and teacher see the selected answer at the same time.

The responses provide the teacher and the student with information about his or her knowledge base, background, feelings, emotions, attitudes, likes or dislikes, facts learned, and misconceptions (see Figure 4.1). During learning experiences the response cards can be designed to reveal feelings and understanding. During a review or cumulating activity, the

Figure 4.1   Example Duo Response Cards

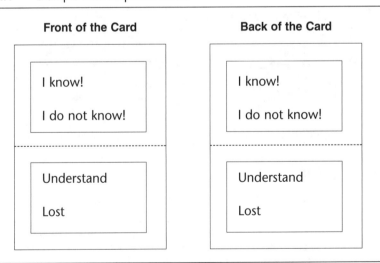

cards can be used as postassessment tools to reveal changes in the student's feelings, attitudes, interests, and academic knowledge.

Sample List of Duo Response Card Possibilities

- I know!
- I understand!
- Agree
- True
- Fact
- Got it!
- Advantage
- I've got it!
- I like this!
- My mind is working!
- I understand!
- I feel great about this!

- I don't know!
- I don't understand!
- Disagree
- False
- Opinion
- No Clue
- Disadvantage
- I don't have a clue!
- I do not like this!
- My mind shut down!
- I am lost!
- This is not working for me!

Triple Responses

Students enjoy the uniqueness of Triple Responses. The cards are designed so the answer choices appear on the front and back (see Figure 4.2). Change the terms often to maintain interest.

Figure 4.2   Example Triple Response Cards

Front	Back
Beginning	Beginning
Middle	Middle
End	End

High to Low Responses

Vary the way responses are listed. The following examples use numbers, words, and phrases that range from high to low. They can be used to quickly learn where students are in their task or in their understanding.

3	2	1
• Happy face	• Straight face	• Sad face
• Yes	• No	• Maybe
• Yes	• No	• Some
• Happy	• So-so	• Sad
• Pluses	• Minuses	• Still questioning
• Explained fully	• Explained some	• Little or no explanation

Low to High Responses

In reverse order, the following number, word, and phrase response samples range from low to high.

1	2	3
• None	• One or two	• Three to five
• Crawling	• Trotting	• Racing
• Need more time	• Checking it over	• Finished
• Questions	• Concerns	• Comments
• Beginning	• Middle	• End

Variation: The Four-Way Response Cards

Modify the directions for the Triple and Duo Responses by adding one more word to the card. Remember to write the same words in the same place on the front and back of the card (see Figure 4.3).

Create a variety of new cards for assessment at different times. Be sure the cards fit the purpose so they show what students know or feel about learning situations and materials.

After a card is made and used the first time, students can add these assessment tools to their personal response card collection.

Content Response Cards

When working with specific content, design response cards as novel, informative tools for assessing learning. Students hold up the response card and point to the answer or the question that applies to a statement. The teacher assesses students according to their quickness and accuracy. Observe students carefully as they prepare to respond. If they appear insecure or hesitant, or if they look to classmates for answers, make a mental or written note. Do not tell them to stop looking at someone else's answer or to turn around. The behavior is a signal that reteaching or review is needed.

The cards can be used with groups of any size across all content areas. Develop response cards to use in any subject. The following examples are for response cards in the science area (see Figure 4.4).

Figure 4.3   Example Four-Way Response Cards

Front/Back	**Front/Back**	**Front/Back**
2	Never	4. I can explain this!
4	Rarely	3. I am beginning to understand.
6	Sometimes	2. I need to ask a question.
8	Often	1. I do not understand.

Figure 4.4   Example Content Response Cards

Science examples:

Front	**Back**
Solid	Solid
Liquid	Liquid
Gas	Gas

The following are examples of content response cards to use with core subject areas:

Science examples:
Three response examples:
- Precipitation
- Evaporation
- Condensation

- Digestive
- Skeletal
- Circulatory

Four response examples:
- Mammal
- Reptile
- Amphibian
- Fish

Social Studies examples:
- North
- South
- East
- West

- Mountain
- Desert
- Prairie
- Plateau

History examples:
- World War I
- World War II
- Both

- Mt. Rushmore
- Liberty Bell
- Statue of Liberty

Language Arts examples:
- Beginning
- Middle
- End

- Period
- Question mark
- Exclamation point

- Setting
- Character
- Plot

- Adjective
- Adverb
- Verb

Math examples:
- Add
- Subtract
- Multiply
- Divide

- Cube
- Cone
- Sphere
- Pyramid

- Penny
- Nickel
- Dime
- Quarter

Show-and-Tell Variations

The prompts below provide varied and inviting ways to spontaneously assess student learning mid-lesson. They are friendlier alternatives to pop quizzes, which are often threatening or punitive. The

Show-and-Tell Variations provide students with opportunities to process learning in different ways while giving teachers data on their levels of understanding.

- Tell a partner
- Say the correct answer together
- Point to the answer or example in one of the following ways:

on a graph	on a bulletin board	on a transparency	in a book
in a passage	in a picture	on a diagram	in the text
in a sentence	in notes	on a chart	on a poster

- Create a sample
- Experiment and discover
- Draw it
- Give an example
- Write it
- Tell it
- Race to the answer on a chart, poster, or board

Take a Stand

The Take a Stand activity preassesses by having students move to a number that represents their knowledge base for a topic or skill. The teacher observes the learners' selected positions to gather information. This assessment activity also includes an analysis of the group discussions.

Directions

A. Place large numbers from one up to six in order around the room. Separate the numbers so there is enough space for a group of students to line up in front of the numbers.
B. Post and state the essential question, standard, fact, topic, or opinion for discussion.
C. Give the following directions to students:
   1. Think about your knowledge of _____.
   2. On a scale of one to six, rate your knowledge of this topic. (Six is the top, or expert, level; one is the lowest, or novice, level.)
   3. Record the rating of your knowledge on a piece of paper.
   4. Stand in front of the number that represents your knowledge level.

5. Discuss why you chose the position with the group.

6. Select a group spokesperson to share the discussion ideas and findings with the class.

Transfer the Take a Stand data into a pictograph by drawing a stick figure to represent each student in each group. This activity gives students opportunities to demonstrate their understandings and reveals misconceptions related to the topic. The discussion information and the student rating chart can be used to plan future lessons.

Note: Use this activity as a preassessment tool by observing the learners' positions on the scale and by listening to group discussions.

Gold Goal Band

The Gold Goal Band activity assesses the students' interests and needs. It teaches students to set personal and academic goals when they are introduced to a new topic or skill. Goals give students a mission, vision, and purpose for the experiences. The goals or objectives are incorporated in lesson plans. The students self-assess their goal attainment and draw a star on the band to signify that their goals have been attained. The teacher observes the completed stars and provides appropriate feedback.

Use the following directions to create the Gold Goal Bands. Cut wide pieces of gold paper into strips that are long enough for each student to make a wristband. Distribute the gold strips of paper. Present the following directions to the group:

Activity: Gold Goal Band

1. Trim the gold paper strip to fit your wrist.

2. Write a goal related to (*insert topic or skill*) on the band.

3. Use a paper clip to place the Gold Goal Band at the top of a page in your portfolio.

4. Write what you need to do next on the paper directly below the band.

5. Draw a large star on the band when you reach your goal.

6. Tape the Gold Goal Band around your wrist to signify that you reached your goal.

Variation: Create a Gold Goal bookmark, miniposter, or pennant.

Knowledge Base Corners

Discover students' content knowledge about a topic before planning a unit or lesson. The Knowledge Base Corners activity is an informal preassessment of students' content knowledge. Use this strategy to introduce upcoming subjects or topics. Introduce students to this activity by using hobbies or sports examples. This shows how everyone varies in their knowledge, interests, and experiences. After students see this strategy modeled several times and become accustomed to using it, they move quickly into the selected corners.

Directions

1. Use four large strips of paper, and label each one with phrases that match the following four-corner grids (see Tables 4.1, 4.2, and 4.3).

2. Post each strip of paper in a corner of the room. Read the names of the corners aloud to the students.

3. Explain that this activity will guide your plans for their instruction.

4. Ask students to write down the name of the corner that matches their response to your question or statement. *Note:* Students will be less likely to change corners to be with friends when they record their choice on paper.

5. Tell students to move to the corner that matches their knowledge level for the topic.

6. Group members give reasons for choosing their corner.
   a. Call on volunteers from each corner.
   b. The group members discuss why they chose the corner. Each group chooses a spokesperson to summarize the key points of the discussion.
   c. Each group selects a recorder to write on chart paper the reason the group members chose the corner. The group decides a novel way to present the information to the rest of the class.

Assessment Note: As students stand in their selected corners, the teacher observes who is on each knowledge level. This information is used to plan the upcoming unit or topic of study.

Assure students who are in the "Not a Clue" corner that with knowledge and experience they can move to the "I've Got It" corner.

Variations: When students know how to use Knowledge Base Corners, add novelty to the activity by changing the phrases on the corner labels.

Table 4.1 Knowledge Base Corners

Corner labels:

Not a clue	I know a *lot!*
I know some.	I've *got* it!

Rookie	Minor League
Amateur	Major League

Table 4.2 Attitude Corners

Students go to the corner that represents their feelings or attitudes toward a topic.

I do not like this.	I like most of it!
I like a few parts.	I like this and cannot wait to learn more.

Table 4.3 Interest Corners

Students go to a corner of the room that matches their level of interest in a topic.

Rarely ever interested	Often interested
Occasionally interested	Interested most of the time

Activity: Mystery Masters

The following preassessment activity reveals the learner's knowledge base and prior experiences related to the topic. The data gathered becomes a major segment of the blueprint for planning differentiated instruction.

Present the students with one to six unfamiliar or unknown bits of information. These can be mystery words, phrases, subtopics, essential questions, key concepts, or events from an upcoming unit or topic of study. Challenge the Mystery Masters to find everything they can about the terms or concepts. Tell the students to scavenge, discover, research, and investigate the meanings, solutions, or ideas associated with the mystery.

Use a Mystery Masters scavenge to create homework activities or Evening Learning Opportunities (ELOs). Give students a week or two to find everything related to the mystery. Provide a place for students to collect the items. Large boxes, tubs, tables, or corner spaces can be used to display the discoveries. Provide an entry log for students to record their contributions to the collection.

Content Knowledge Boxes

To uncover what students know and to identify misconceptions they may have, use preassessment activities before beginning a content study unit. Use content boxes to identify the entry points for planning instruction (see Table 4.4).

Example

Country _____

We will learn about the areas listed on the chart during our study of the country of _____.

Complete the chart with information you know about the country of _____. If you do not know specific facts, write your thoughts about each category.

Content Surveys

Content Surveys provide the background and knowledge base of an individual or group of students. Assess students one to three weeks before the unit is planned so the information can be incorporated during the planning process. Effective surveys or intriguing questionnaires include activities such as Mystery Words and Mystery Concepts. Content Surveys

Table 4.4 Content Knowledge Boxes

Location	Food, Clothing, and Shelter	Economy and Jobs
Government	Population and People	Ways of Life and Customs

Variation 1:

Country _____

Geography	Economy	Government	Ways of Life

Variation 2:

Compare Countries

United States of America	(Country of Study)

are effective preassessment tools when they uncover what students know about an upcoming study.

Teacher-created inventories and surveys are best. These assessment tools can be brief and provide needed information. Use surveys as data-gathering tools every month or two. Ask questions about the specific topic. Include questions and statements that delve into the student's background knowledge, past experiences with the subject, and expectations or goals related to the learning.

Develop Questions and Statements for Surveys

Example: Preassessment Survey

We will learn about _____.

How does _____ relate to you?

What do you know about _____?

How do you feel about _____?

What do you want to learn about _____?

Personal Inventories and Surveys

Personal inventories and surveys provide information about the life of a student. They provide information about the student's knowledge background and prior experiences, interests, emotions, feelings, likes, dislikes, dreams, and goals. These factors have a direct impact on a student's approach to learning, engagement, and level of performance.

Brainstorming

Use brainstorming to give students a voice. Use questions similar to the following to gather data related to what the students already know about a standard, concept, topic, or unit of study.

- List the terms, facts, or concepts you know about our new topic.
- What experiences have you had with the information?
- Have you heard about this subject in other classes? When and where?
- What have you studied that would compare to this subject?
- List books or articles that relate to the information.
- What do you think the author is going to share about the topic?
- List the differences between this topic and _____.
- Share information you have about the topic.

- How have you used this information?
- What do you predict about the new material?

Note: Remember to tell students to write their individual responses before sharing them with a group.

Color Clusters

The following Color Cluster activity uses a color key to identify students' levels of knowledge related to a topic. Give each student a set or cluster of colored disks made from construction paper to match a key similar to the one below. Ask each student to display the color that reflects his or her level of learning of a particular skill or topic.

Example Key

Purple = On the launchpad

Yellow = Cautious

Green = Moving on up

Blue = Soaring

Red = Full speed ahead

Variation: Ask students to place the disks in their desks or to keep them in an accessible place. Ask them to show the color that reflects their feelings about a topic or task.

Gallimaufry Gatherings

This ELO activity not only activates and assesses prior knowledge but also develops interest in an upcoming topic or unit of study through anticipation and curiosity. Students create a mental organizer for new knowledge to come. Assign this activity a week or two before the study begins.

Tell students they are going to create a topic or unit gallimaufry, or hodgepodge, of various things. Place the topic on the outside of a box, bucket, tub, crate, or shelf. Challenge students to become scavengers, discoverers, and investigators to find the solutions and answers to a posed problem or question related to the upcoming topic, person, or event. Encourage the learners to fill the container with written materials related to the topic.

Learners find the resources or information in various media, across many genres. Some ways to find information are through interviews, magazine articles, newspaper clippings, on the World Wide Web, or on television. The teacher and students need to screen the material for accuracy. Create an entry form for students to complete when they contribute to the collection (see Figure 4.5). The collection enhances the learning atmosphere as students develop a feeling of ownership in the new learning experience. Use the collection as a resource to enhance the unit of study.

The Gallimaufry Gathering activity, and similar preassessment tools, are designed to do the following:

- Develop interest in the topic
- Involve students in the search
- Give learners responsibility and ownership in gathering the information
- Develop a resource reference collection
- Increase background knowledge on the upcoming topic
- Create curiosity and build anticipation

Figure 4.5   Gallimaufry Gathering Grid

NAME _____

TOPIC _____

1. I found
2. It tells
3. We can use it to
Signature: _____   Date: _____   Resources: _____

As students engage in the activity, their knowledge base expands. They build a foundation for learning with each discovery. Students become responsible for their own learning as they actively participate in preparations for the new topic of study. The hype accompanying this activity creates curiosity. Anticipation builds until the topic has its premiere. Create opportunities for students to share the results of their discoveries.

FORMAL PREASSESSMENT

Using a variety of formal and informal preassessment tools shows what the learner knows prior to the study. These instruments can be used to preassess and then be used again for postassessment as a formal measure of the learning that has taken place.

Developing the Pretest

Adapt the following guidelines to create a pretest. Keep in mind that a pretest should reflect the learners' strengths as it identifies their needs. It takes time to strategically develop a pretest, however; it is a valuable tool when the findings guide differentiated instruction.

Administer the preassessment two weeks before teaching the new topic or unit.

1. Design the test items so no one can achieve a score of 100 percent. Be sure the items challenge every student taking the test.

2. Design the items so no one receives a score of 0 percent.

3. Plan the test to cover the full range of learning, from the simple to the complex.

4. Present items that range from hands-on to abstract.

5. Disperse easy and difficult questions or tasks throughout the assessment. This deters students from assuming that the easiest portion of the assessment is at the beginning. Often students stop trying when they come to a difficult question because they assume the remaining tasks will be even more difficult.

6. Include manipulatives in the preassessment if they are used in related lessons.

7. Use the same pre- and posttest to analyze growth.

Vary the formats of the pretest. For example, use open-ended questions, graphic organizers, matching, multiple choice, and fill in the blank.

Design the items to challenge learners with different levels of questions and thinking.

ASSESSMENT DURING LEARNING

The ongoing gathering of information related to the student's progress during the learning is essential. This is the time to plan strategically to reteach, readjust, revamp, enhance, or enrich according to the diverse needs of the learners. Continuous quality assessments with interventions avoid pitfalls and struggles that discourage and lead to failure.

The following unique assessment strategies and activities are designed to excite and stimulate the student's mind.

Baggie Tools

Use the following Baggie Tool ideas as unique ways to assess students as they are learning. Provide each student with a "baggie" to store their personal assessment tools. After tools are made and used, students add them to the baggie collection. Remind students to collect tools throughout the year. When students need to use a specific assessment strategy, they use the appropriate handy Baggie Tool. For example, when using a multiple-choice activity, each student uses an "ABCD" response card.

The following list provides samples of collectible assessment tools:

response cards	game pieces	stickers	stars	disks
self-stick notes	self-stick flags	markers	highlighters	rulers
pen lights	tongue depressors	Popsicle sticks	fake fingers	dots

assessment cards   small strips of colored transparency paper

Game Pieces

The following section provides various ways to use game pieces for assessment. Gather spare board pieces or disks from games such as Monopoly or Clue. Ask parents to donate pieces from games that are no longer used. Give each student some red and green houses from the Monopoly game. Here are a few examples of various ways to use these game pieces for assessment:

- Place the green houses on statements in the passages that give information, the definition, attributes, or details about the words. Share the findings with a partner, a small group, or the entire class.

- Place the red house on the main idea. Place a small green house on each supporting detail.
- Place a green house on each example in the chapter that fits the new concept.

Note: If green and red houses are not available, use two other objects to identify main ideas and supporting details.

Cash In

Use a roll of cash register tape. As the tape is passed around the group, each student takes a turn writing three words from the story or content on the paper. The next person adds three words that connect with the ongoing story. Contributing students place their initials beside their three written words.

A Bump in the Road

The student writes a problem he or she has with the learning at the top of a piece of paper and passes it to three to five classmates to obtain their suggestions. Each person initials his or her suggestion(s).

Sticky Tabs

Cut a sticky note into smaller tabs. These markers create unique assessment tools that are easy to observe as students engage in tasks. The following activity is an example of how Sticky Tabs are used to find the mystery word, meaning, character, fact, step, or rule:

1. Locate the mystery _____.

2. Find three ways the _____ is used.

3. Place a tab on each example.

Observe and Assess

- Was the student accurate in locating each example?
- Was he or she able to find the information and tab it quickly?

Dots, Stickers, and Stars

The following activity uses dots, stickers, or stars in skimming and scanning for important words or information:

1. Review the notes you wrote in class.

2. Locate important points, words, or phrases in a chapter or passage.

3. Identify each important point by placing a sticker, dot, or star on it.

Observe and Assess

- Were the student's choices and selections of important components correct?
- Did the student exhibit confidence in making the choices?
- What would improve this learner's skills, strategies, and speed in finding information?

Double Duty

The Double Duty activity can be used to record important information (see Figure 4.6). Create numbers using wide double lines. Students write their responses to Number 1 inside the numeral or around it.

Variations

- Use the Double Duty activity to compare words, topics, or objects.
- Draw the numbers 1, 2, and 3 with double lines to respond to three questions.
- Draw a question mark using double lines. Write a question, concern, or the answer to a question inside the question mark.
- Draw a large exclamation point using double lines to create a writing space inside it.
- Students respond to the following prompt: My "Aha!" for today is . . .

Figure 4.6   Double Duty

Musical Notes

Students enjoy applying music to self-assessments. Challenge students to select theme songs or musical instruments to accompany the study topics, and have them explain why they link the tune to the learning.

Use the following list of examples to demonstrate how to select appropriate theme songs to express understanding of a topic:

Songs	Why?
"Celebrate"	Because I've "got it!"
"I Can See Clearly Now"	Because I understand the information
"Leaving on a Jet Plane!"	Because I am "soaring" with this idea.

INSTRUCTIONAL STRATEGIES AS ASSESSMENT TOOLS

Taking Notes

Note-taking skills do not come naturally to learners. Often adults take this ability for granted, assuming that students understand the thinking processes that accompany note taking. Often students do not understand the benefit, rationale, purpose, and value of taking notes.

These skills must be explicitly taught and modeled routinely during lectures, discussions, readings, demonstrations, and activities. The teacher usually writes notes for the whole class to view, displaying them on the board, a chart, a computer monitor, or an overhead. When modeling note-taking skills, students need to hear the teacher's inside thinking or self-talk.

Add novelty to note taking to improve the students' ability to remember important information. When a unique reference mark is used, key points are easier to remember and retain.

Examples

- Highlight important terms or key ideas.
- Tab important or confusing sections of text.
- Write questions or confusions on self-stick notes, and bookmark the place.
- Draw a box to enclose each key item.
- Place an asterisk, star, or check mark beside important items, such as key names, dates, events, or terms.
- Circle a key idea.

- Draw an exclamation point next to the most important facts, such as "George Washington was the first president of the United States!"
- Place a question mark before a confusing word, phrase, or sentence.
- Write the following responses in notes to highlight important pieces for future study:

WOW	OK	YES	Got it
No clue	Duh!	Help	Lost

Color Coding

Use color coding to identify steps in a procedure, to organize an agenda, or to highlight items in a list. Involve students in selecting the order of the colors in the sequence. School colors may be used as the first two colors. This helps students remember the beginning sequence. Post the color sequence. Maintain the same color scheme throughout the year. When a school establishes a color-coding sequence, the visual become a guide for the entire student body to remember rules or general procedures.

Example: 1 = black   2 = blue   3 = green   4 = red   5 = purple

- Color-code with markers, crayons, colored pencils, or construction paper.
- Choose the color to identify the most important information.
- Choose the color to identify the least important information.
- Write each step of a procedure using colored pencils or pens to match the key.

Color Overlays

Place a clear, colored transparency over a page of print to assist students as they read information. The color overlay removes glare from a page like a pair of sunglasses. Some students have reported that the color keeps the words from appearing to move on the page. Extensive research on the use of color with reading materials was conducted by Marie Carbo, a learning styles expert. Use a colored, transparent clipboard as an overlay when reading a book or other written material (Carbo, 1986). Sunglasses with rose, blue, or yellow lenses will also work.

Design Delights

Have students choose a favorite shape or symbol that makes a connection with information from the unit or topic of study. Students decorate the outline of the shape by recording key points on and around it.

Sketches From the Mind

Have students use simple, miniature drawings from the unit or topic of study to mark important facts or concepts. The drawings provide a mental picture or symbol to locate and remember information.

Examples

1. In a unit on food study, draw an apple beside each important fact related to fruit.

2. In a transportation unit with the categories *land, sea,* and *air,* draw a road beside land vehicles; draw waves beside sea vehicles; and draw a cloud beside air vehicles. If the vehicle fits more than one category, use each symbol that matches.

Variation: Label it!

L for land   *S* for sea   *A* for air

1. In a math unit that teaches process and procedures, place the operational symbol, such as +, −, ×, or ÷, beside the steps.

SELF-TALK

Self-talk is internal dialogue or thinking that takes place in an individual's mind as he or she analyzes questions, works through problems, or processes information. The purpose of self-talk is to raise the student's level of consciousness related to his or her own thinking. It is a learning tool to use during instruction. It is also a strategy to stimulate recall during assessments. Teach effective self-talk. Model, model, and model again the inside thinking that occurs as you use this tool in daily lessons.

Use the following opportunities to model self-talk:

- To explain the sequence of a procedure
- To follow directions
- To explain the thinking process for solving a problem

Self-Talk to Process Information

Students need to become aware of the value of self-talk as they engage in learning activities and assessments.

Examples

- This is my inside thinking.
- I will explain my step-by-step thinking for this procedure.
- Listen as I bring my inside thinking outside!
- I think this goes right here. Does that make sense to me?
- Now I need to _____.
- Is this fact important? Why?
- I need to write this down!

Keep in mind that a major goal of assessment is for students to know how to engage in self-assessment in all subject areas and in their daily activities. They can learn to assess their thinking during a process by writing their steps in thinking, telling a partner, or discussing it with a small group. Practice in using metacognitive skills teaches students to organize their thoughts, understand their thinking processes, and express themselves reflectively. When students understand and productively use self-talk, they have a valuable tool at their fingertips to use in all subjects and throughout life.

Activity: The Brain's Speech Bubble

Use the following activity to introduce and model self-talk. Students will see how well it works. The speech bubble represents the self-talk so that students can see their own inside thinking processes.

1. Make a large speech bubble.

2. Select a student to act as the speaker, or have the teacher explain his or her inside thinking while solving a problem.

3. Each time the person tells his or her thinking for a step, the bubble is held directly above the speaker's head. The speaker stands beneath the Brain's Speech Bubble as he or she verbalizes the brain's thinking for the class.

4. The speaker moves away from the speech bubble when not voicing his or her inside thinking to the class.

The speaker may use the following self-talk examples while standing beneath the Brain's Speech Bubble. Step to the side to explain the brain's thinking on each question. Introduce the questions for self-talk during and after assessments. Self-talk examples are used throughout this book.

Before

- Is my mind focused on the task?
- Do I have what I need to get started?
- How do I get started?
- How can I organize my thoughts?

During

- Am I following directions?
- Does my answer make sense right here?
- Do I need a new category?
- Am I placing each piece of information in the right category?

Note: When students understand how to use self-talk for an assessment activity, challenge them to create and model self-talk in their next assignments.

By using multiple assessments before and during learning, the teacher is aware of individual strengths and weaknesses and can plan and adapt instruction to meet those needs. Ongoing assessment also provides constructive feedback to students and leads them to develop habits of metacognition and self-monitoring for their own learning.

Assessing After 5
the Learning

Essential Question: How can various differentiated assessment strategies be used to identify immediate and future instructional needs of learners?

Assessing after the learning has traditionally been viewed as a way to analyze the student's mastery of the standards. Postassessments are a crucial step because the results are analyzed to see if the learner has reached the initial goals. If the goals have not been reached, specific plans are customized for this individual. A teacher uses many forms of assessment to determine whether some or all students need additional experiences in one or more aspects of a unit before the formal assessment. This chapter includes both formal and informal tools for use at various after-learning junctures at the end of a lesson or instructional segment.

◆

EFFECTIVE QUESTIONING TECHNIQUES FOR ASSESSMENT

Open-Ended Questions

Open-ended questions challenge students to think and choose their thoughts for the responses. For example, the teacher provides a situation, and the student communicates his or her thoughts and ideas in an answer. It may be in the form of an essential question, hypothesis, or statement. The answer has many details, an explanation, or a process. This is an important part of assessment. If a student uses correct information in a response, he or she shows what is known about the topic. The answer reflects the student's views and opinions and shows the student's ability to explain the facts or supporting details. Use the following examples of open-ended questions:

Explain how . . .   What is your opinion of . . . ?

What is the reason . . . ?   Describe . . .

Tell more about . . .   Tell your step-by-step thinking on . . .

How did you solve this problem?   What happened next?

How can you use the information?

Students may be unable to answer open-ended questions because they do not understand the terms in the directions. Provide time for them to discuss and use the most common terms used in assessment activities. Explain these Words for the Wise, or key words, in terms students can understand. For example, a student-friendly definition for *analyze* is "dig in with details" (Chapman & King, 2003b). Teach students to use questions for self-analysis and reflection. Incorporate questions similar to the following in daily lessons and discussions to teach students how to apply this skill in routine assessments.

Examples: Throughout the day, week, or assignment . . .

- How many adjustments or changes did you make? Tell me about one of them.
- What obstacles did you overcome?
- What discoveries have you made?
- How will you do this differently the next time?
- Describe the easiest part.
- Describe your least favorite part.
- Tell about the most enjoyable part of the assessment activity.

The following prompts also lead students to become self-reflective:

- A problem I solved today was _____.
- Here is the step-by-step way I solved the problem:
- Draw a picture, tell or write . . .

  To show what you learned

  To show what you need next

  To show what you would do differently next time

  To reflect your feelings about the assessment

  To show what you did during assessment

Sample Student Questions to Use After the Learning

These open-ended questions are used with journals, discussions, or tests while working with content of a specific topic or unit.

1. What is the most important thing I learned?

2. How can I explain it?

3. What was the most difficult part?

4. What was the easiest part?

5. What do I need to learn next?

6. If I could have done one thing differently, what would it have been?

7. Do I have any other comments?

Lead-ins: Reflection Reactions

Use the following questions as an assessment tool for self-analysis and self-reflection at the end of a week, an assignment, a unit, a class period, or an activity:

- Explain the adjustments you made.
- List the obstacles you had to overcome.
- Discuss the compromises you made.
- Describe your discoveries.
- How will you do this differently next time?
- What was the easiest part?
- Write a paragraph about the most meaningful thing you learned.
- Describe your least favorite part of this activity.
- What was the most enjoyable activity?
- A problem I solved today was _____.
- Here are the step-by-step ways I solved the problem:
- Draw a picture, tell, or write about _____ . . .

  To reflect your feelings today

  To show what you did today during

  To show what you learned

  To show what you need to learn next

  To illustrate how you would do it differently next time

Inadequate Response

1 = No attempt to answer

2 = Begins, but is unable to complete answer

Satisfactory Response

3 = Minor flaws, but satisfactory answer

Demonstrated Competence

4 = Competent Response

5 = Exemplary Response

BLOOM'S TAXONOMY FOR COMPREHENSION ASSESSMENT

Use effective questioning as probes to reveal information the student knows and to identify information he or she needs to learn. Use the following key words to develop probing statements, prompts, and questions at various levels of thinking as identified by Bloom and Krathwohl (1956).

Evaluation

Judge the quality	Determine the value	Rate
Assess	Evaluate	Appraise	Estimate the worth

- Appraise (criticize, conclude) _____ .
- Describe the value of this law.
- Evaluate the impact of the new product on family life.

Synthesis

Compose	Propose	Formulate	Assemble	Construct
Design	Arrange	Organize	Prepare	Plan

- Compose (rearrange, compile) _____ .
- Use the separate components to create a new product.
- Arrange the details to develop a _____ .

Analysis

Examine	Distinguish	Question	Differentiate	Diagram
	Criticize	Experiment	Identify	

- Outline (categorize, separate) _____ .
- What are the steps in the procedure?
- What might happen next?
- How do you prove the hypothesis?

Application

Demonstrate	Practice	Interview	Apply	Translate
Dramatize	Operate	Schedule	Illustrate	Interpret

- Demonstrate (operate, show) _____ .
- How can you use _____ ?
- What ideas and facts support this _____ ?

Comprehension

Describe	Restate	Explain	Identify	Report	
Compare	Discuss	Recognize	Express	Locate	Review

- Explain (estimate, summarize) _____ .
- Describe _____ .
- How do you view this _____ ?
- What is the author saying?

Knowledge

Define	List	Repeat	Memorize	Name	Label
Record	Recall	Relate	Tell	Report	Narrate

- Define (recall, recite) _____ .
- What is _____ ?
- What is the purpose?

OBSERVABLE BEHAVIOR

Teachers conduct formal and informal observations for the following basic purposes:

- To identify students who know how to use the new information so they can move on, add to, and enhance learning.
- To identify students who need reteaching, reviewing, or more background information.
- To identify how a student approaches and solves problems and explains their solutions.

The following section presents practical ways to record data gathered during observations.

Tallies

Use tallies to record the number of students, partners, or small groups who successfully master a skill and to record those who need more assistance. Use the following guidelines to create tallies on a graph:

- As students, partners, or a small group show success, place a check mark or a tally mark beside the skill or task.
- Label small groups as A, B, C, and D. When the behavior or skill is successfully performed, place the group's corresponding letter next to the appropriate behavior (see Figures 5.1 and 5.2).

Figure 5.1   Tally Table

(Standard or Skill)

	Team A	Team B	Team C	Team D
Standard	ᴜᴜ	II	III	ᴜᴜ II
Standard	II	IIII	ᴜᴜ	II

Observable Behavior, Skill, or Standard

Performed Successfully

1.	
2.	
3.	
4.	

Figure 5.2   Observation Chart

Use the following chart to record student behaviors as they are learning a standard. This form is an excellent tool for keeping logs or records over time.

Student _____   **Standard** _____

Observer _____

Observation 1
Date

BUS STOP CENTER

Create a Bus Stop Center, or checking station, as a designated area where students can check their work with a grading key. Provide directions and the answer key for students to use to check their own papers. Include specific directions that tell students where to turn in their corrected work.

Stock the station with answer keys, colored pens, answer sheets, and labeled baskets. Vary the directions. The student enters the Bus Stop to correct his work. The only writing implements allowed at the station are the ones placed there by the teacher.

Variations:

Example: The checker chooses three colored pens and completes a marking key similar to the following:

Green = My corrections!

Purple = My opinion!

Yellow = Spotlights my best work on this assignment!

Match the special checking tools with the topic of study. For example, in a study of plants, supply green gel pens to represent growth. In a study of historical documents, attach a feather to represent a quill.

The Bus Stop Center reduces the amount of paperwork for the teacher to grade. The greatest value of the center, however, is for the student to view his or her areas of strength, to actively engage in self-correcting responses, and to receive immediate feedback. As students take responsibility for checking and marking their work during the checking process, they develop confidence and a sense of independence, learn to self-assess, and move in the direction of becoming self-regulated learners.

Challenge students to choose or create another name for the Bus Stop Center, as in the following examples:

- Correct Spot
- Correction Zone
- Is That Your Final Answer?
- Blemish-Remover Zone
- Survivor Checkpoint

Reward students with opportunities to become the next Bus Stop Center helper, checker, or analyst. When students become productive in using the station, challenge them to design a new checking key and to select special tools for the station.

ELOs

Evening Learning Opportunities (ELOs) are afterschool challenges that reinforce or support learning. The term *ELO* produces more positive feelings about learning than the term *homework*. Use ELOs to engage students in activities that require higher-order thinking skills. The goal of using ELOs is for students to apply understandings of terms, facts, and concepts to their daily routines and activities. Students are detectives, scavengers, investigators, and inventors as they complete ELO assignments.

ELO Examples From Content Areas

Math

- Name items in your kitchen that are packaged in pint, quart, gallon, or liter containers.
- Find a recipe that uses a tablespoon, a teaspoon, and a cup to measure ingredients. Bring a copy of the recipe to class to share.
- Find examples of the following shapes in your neighborhood: circles, squares, triangles, and ovals. Make a list of the items with the names of the shapes they represent.

Science

- Create a drawing to show how you classify or organize your clothes, free time activities, toys, books, and DVDs.
- Make a chart to show the categories of food in your kitchen or items in your garage.
- List animals found in your neighborhood and home. Label them as mammals, fish, birds, reptiles, or amphibians.

Physical Education

- Observe a baseball, football, basketball, or soccer team. Compare and contrast the major strengths and weaknesses, specific skills, or sportsmanship exhibited.
- If you participate in a sport, list the activities you engage in to get ready for a game in sequential order.

Social Studies

- Interview a parent, neighbors, or others about the requirements for their jobs. Identify their skills and work habits.
- Review a movie or documentary based on the country you are studying. Create a chart to show the advantages and disadvantages of living in that country.

Language Arts

- Watch a sitcom, newscast, or reality show. Record the main ideas and supporting details.
- Watch a game show, or play a game. Write the sequence of events.

LIKERT SCALES TO ASSESS LEARNING, ATTITUDE, AND PROGRESS

A Likert scale comprises a line with graduated numbers, ascending or descending. An individual's level of performance is assessed using the descriptors for each number on the scale. To create novel scales, use words or phrases that indicate progress on the scale, and share these with students.

Workable Likert Scales to Assess Learning and Attitudes

Introduce Likert scales to students. Vary the number sequences and terms on the lines, so the users will be alert to specific directions each time they use the assessment tools (see Figures 5.3 and 5.4).

Figure 5.3   Workable Likert Scales to Assess Learning and Attitudes

1. Use numbers to depict score.

| 2 | 4 | 6 | 8 |

| 8 | 6 | 4 | 2 |

2. Use words that fit the age of the student, the tone or mood, progress, and feelings about the topic of study to plot the score. For example:

| Starting Line | Making a Lap | Racing Full Throttle | Finish Line |

3. Use words or phrases along a continuum that is designed to fit the student's age, the standard, or the task being assessed. Mark the scale according to the learner's knowledge base.

| Knows very little | Knows some | Knows most of this | Knows this! |

| No! | | Maybe! | | Yes! |

| Rarely ever | A little | Often | A favorite |

4. Place an "X" on the line that reflects an observable behavior.

| Little or no involvement | Some involvement | Involved most of the time | Involved completely |

RUBRICS: ROAD MAPS TO EXPECTATIONS

Introduce learners to the word *rubric*. It is derived from the Latin word *rubrica*, which means "red." Show students a ruby stone, if one is available. Explain that the earliest uses of the word *rubric* referred to a title, heading, or important passage that appeared in red letters to distinguish it from the less important information.

Figure 5.4   Progress Likert Scale. Use a Likert scale to monitor progress on a project, contract, or activity.

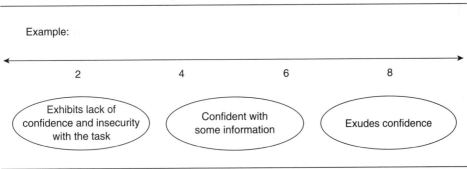

Rubrics commonly used in classrooms today provide the teacher, the student, and parents with the important details for assessment. Each rubric contains an outlined scale. Traditional rubrics contain three to five-point scales. The expectations for a specific task are indicated by the numbers on the scale. The indicators or explanations beside each number on the scale must be clear so the student understands them. They must be concise so the teacher can use them to assess student work.

The best rubrics are created by the teacher, and they measure what is taught. When it is feasible, students should participate in designing the rubrics. Rubrics can be customized to assess specific content knowledge, writing, listening skills, behaviors, tasks, responsibilities, oral presentations, projects, demonstrations, or teamwork (see Figures 5.5, 5.6, and 5.7).

Rubric Hodgepodge

Why not create a Rubric Hodgepodge, a collection of rubrics that vary in formats, scales, and indicators? Teachers often rely on their formal knowledge of well-known rubrics to develop a scale when they are planning a specific assignment. If a handy collection of ideas is readily available, the rubric developer is more likely to include all appropriate areas.

Build this Rubric Hodgepodge by collecting rubrics you have used or those that have been shared with you. The collection becomes a ready reference when you need to identify the specific descriptors for the levels of success.

The four-quadrant rubric may need to be reduced or expanded to accommodate the individual's specific needs or the level of the task. The tool must fit the criteria and include the appropriate indicators. The goal is to provide the learner with the best instrument possible to show the most complete assessment picture. By sharing these with students at the beginning of learning, teachers help them become more successful. The indicators present students with clear learning goals and benchmarks for success.

(Text continues on page 107)

Figure 5.5   Rubric Form Samples

Rubric Form Sample I

Name _____   Assignment _____   Date _____

Assessor: _____   Teacher _____   Self   _____ Peer

Criterion _____

$$1 \longleftrightarrow 5$$

| 1 | 3 | 5 |

Comments

Indicators

_____   _____   _____

_____   _____   _____

_____   _____   _____

Rubric Form Sample II

Student _____   Project _____

Assessor: _____   Self _____ Teacher _____ Peer

Project or product title	1	2	3	4	Score
Criteria	Descriptor Descriptor Descriptor	Descriptor Descriptor Descriptor	Descriptor Descriptor Descriptor	Descriptor Descriptor Descriptor	
Criteria	Descriptor Descriptor Descriptor	Descriptor Descriptor Descriptor	Descriptor Descriptor Descriptor	Descriptor Descriptor Descriptor	

Total Score _____

Comments

Figure 5.6   More Rubric Form Samples and Rubric for a Group Project

Content Area: Science
Topic: Digestive System
Task: Design a display that explains major functions of the digestive system

Name _____

Criteria	Full plate, 4	All but dessert, 3	Still hungry, 2	Missed the dinner bell, 1
Layout	The display is organized and attractive	The display is appealing. Each part is easy to view	The display is disorganized. Some parts difficult to see	The display is disorganized and unattractive
Accuracy of Content	Information on all four functions is accurate	Most of the information on the four functions is correct	A few details and some of the information is accurate	Information on all four functions is incorrect
Completeness of Content	All four functions are identified and fully described in an organized format. Detailed descriptions of each function and the interrelationships among them are included	All four functions are identified and contain some organization. The descriptions use incomplete details	Two or three functions are described using a few details. The content is disorganized	All functions are not identified. Descriptions of the functions are incomplete and totally disorganized
Diagrams/ Graphics	The graphic designs are creative, organized, and clearly explain the topic	Each graphic helps explain the topic and is easy to understand	A few graphics are appropriate and explain the topic	The graphics are unclear. They do not add understanding to the display
Use of Resources	Five or more resources support the information presented	Three or four resources appropriately support the information	One or two appropriate resources were used	No resources were used to support the information
Teamwork	Worked extremely well with others on all parts of the project as a valuable team member	Got along well with the team. Shared in most responsibilities	Occasionally interfered with the team's work. Permitted others to complete most of the work	Did not work as a responsible team member on the project
Using the Guidelines	Stayed on task. Followed all directions and guidelines	Worked successfully with minimum disruptions to the assignment work	Occasional off-task behaviors interfered with the team's work quality	Off-task behaviors and disruptions interfered with the team's task

(Continued)

Figure 5.6 (Continued)

Rubric Form Sample III

Student _____   Grade _____   Topic _____

Standard _____

$\longleftarrow$ _____ $\longrightarrow$

        Not Yet   Some   Got It!

Standard _____

$\longleftarrow$ _____ $\longrightarrow$

        Not Yet   Some   Got It!

Comments

Understands	Working on	Needs Help

Rubric Form Sample IV

Task _____

Behavior Indicators: What am I assessing and observing?

Student Names	Behavior A	Behavior B	Behavior C
1.			
2.			
3.			

Rubric Form Sample V

Student _____   Class/Subject _____   Date _____

Assignment _____

8	Expert _____ _____ _____
6	Knows most of it! _____ _____ _____
4	Knows some information _____ _____ _____
2	Novice _____ _____ _____

(Continued)

Figure 5.6 (Continued)

Sample Rubric Headings to Describe Success Levels

Does not understand	Can complete task with assistance	Can do some alone	Works independently

1–2 correct	3–5 correct	6–8 correct	9–10 correct

Novice	Apprentice	Approaching mastery	Expert

Encounter	Engage	Enhance	Embrace

Little or no knowledge	Knows some	Knows a lot	Knows this well

Novice	Apprentice	Journeyman	Master

At the beginning	Completed some	Completed most	Completed all

Rarely ever	Sometimes	Often	Most of the time

Can do very little	Can do some	Knows how to do most of the task	Knows how to complete the task

Does not like this	Likes it some	Enjoys this most of the time	Loves It! A favorite!

Afraid of this task	Some comfort	Comfortable most of the time	Fearlessly approached this task and comfortably completed it

Dirt road	Paved road	Highway	Yellow brick road

Not a clue	Beginning to understand it	Understands most of it	Got It!

It takes more time to develop an effective rubric than it takes to score it. Rubrics are very effective tools because they clarify the teacher's expectations. These effective tools make it easy to adapt and differentiate assessment because the content and design can be varied for a specific activity, for a group of students, or for an individual learner.

Use novelty in the rubric design. Vary the format and the content to maintain interest and challenge students. For example, if the rubric is usually presented in the form of horizontal boxes, use vertical boxes. Once students know how to use a scale with drawings, use a scale with numbers. When students know how to use a numbered scale successfully, try using a scale with words. Vary the order of the scales from high to low and low to high so learners realize they must read directions carefully before they begin. Also be aware that it may take some students longer than others to master a particular scale format. Invite learners to design their own rubrics, or "rubricate," for self-evaluation during independent assignments and activities.

Fully constructed rubrics using this sample format that have been built to include a full set of criteria and descriptors are frequently used to assess a culminating unit project or other substantial student-work product. In these instances students benefit tremendously from having the rubric in their hands at the outset so they know the specific descriptors of success, as in the following example.

Progress Rubric

Use a scale similar to the previous one to complete the progress rubric in Figure 5.7.

Figure 5.7   Progress rubric

	Organization	Accuracy	Progress
3rd day			
5th day			
7th day			

Weighted Rubrics

A weighted rubric contains a graduated scoring scale. Each number on the scale contains a brief description of the tasks expected and the level of performance. The highest number on the scale usually has a description of high-quality expectations. The lowest number usually contains a description of the lowest task quality and performance that is accepted in the assignment. This gives each number a weight or value. When learners know the weight or value of each number on the scale, they know the criteria expected. They understand the quality of performance required for each scaled number before their work begins. Weighted rubrics take subjectivity out of the grading process. They help make assessment fair to everyone. All learners have the opportunity to make a high score.

In the following example of a weighted rubric, the criteria and expectations are listed for each number on the four-point scale.

Weighted Rubric for a Biographical Essay

4 points

The writer does the following:
- Thoroughly describes the individual from his or her own point of view
- Uses detailed descriptions of two to three of the person's contributions to society
- Uses three or more references from the text or other sources to add support

3 points

The writer does the following:

- Adequately describes the individual using a few details and explanations
- Briefly describes one or two of the individual's contributions to society
- Uses two references from the text and other sources to add support

2 points

The writer does the following:

- Uses few details to describe the individual
- Provides incomplete explanations of the individual's contributions to society
- Uses one reference from the text or other sources to add support

Using Rubrics for Independent Work

Use the rubric assessment scale in Figure 5.8 while a student is individually engaged in an assignment at a center, experiment, lab, station, or computer.

Figure 5.8 Rubrics for Independent Work

Name _____ Date _____

Working on _____

1. Time on Task

Little or no time on task	Stays on task with adult supervision	Stays on task most of the time	Stays on task until task is completed

2. Gets to work immediately

Does not start immediately	Slowly becomes busy	Tackles a task immediately

3. Works alone

Needs major assistance	Needs some assistance	Works at his or her own pace

4. Attitude toward working alone

$$\longleftarrow \qquad\qquad\qquad\qquad\qquad\qquad \longrightarrow$$

2	4	6	8

Negative   Positive

Comments

(Assessor's) Signature _____ Date _____

CHECKLISTS

Checklists itemize standards, skills, or behaviors to observe or monitor for a specific purpose. The best checklists are created by the teacher, because he or she knows the areas that need to be assessed. These tools are easily customized to meet the needs of the teacher and the student.

The time and energy expended in developing checklists is worthwhile when the tools gather valuable data, provide feedback, and focus instruction on the individual learner's needs.

Use checklists with the following:

- New learning as a process to identify steps completed, understood, or performed
- Behavior management to observe and collect data as a student participates in individual or group experiences
- Centers, projects, experiments, and demonstrations to assess academic needs, on-task behavior, and social interactions

Developing a Checklist

Checklists are practical, flexible assessment tools because they can be designed for a specific subject, activity, skill, or behavior. These instruments can be used during routine activities, transition periods, and special events. The most valuable checklists assess a learner's skills, knowledge, and attitudes to develop instructional plans.

Adapt the following steps to develop checklists:

1. Choose the purpose of the checklist.

2. Identify the learner(s) to monitor.

3. Brainstorm and list all possibilities to produce a quantity of items.

4. Write each item for the checklist on a separate self-stick note.

5. Reduce the list from quantity to quality items.

6. Select the best form to use.

7. Place the quality items in order on the form.

8. Decide who will observe and record the scores. Usually the observer is the teacher, a peer, or an assistant. Include a signature line for each observer.

Checklist for the Checklist

Use the following checklist to analyze the format and the contents of the checklist assessment tool.

- Contains observable, clear, specific items
- Uses a format that is easy to score
- Provides only needed data
- Includes a key
- Contains space for the student name, assessor signature, and date completed by self, peer, small group, teacher, or observer
- Adapts to observations of individual, partners, small groups, or whole class
- Shows growth over a period of time
- Includes spaces for comments

When multiple observers complete a checklist for one student, compile the checklist results to produce a more complete view of the learner. If possible, give the student responsibility for completing the checklist too (see Figures 5.9 and 5.10).

Checklist for Independent Work

Teach students how to use the following checklist by sharing the "inner speech" or self-talk needed to respond to each question. Model and practice the use of the checklist before giving it as independent work.

Sample Checklist for Independent Work

Yes	No	
☐	☐	Do I understand the purpose of this assignment?
☐	☐	Do I know what to do?
☐	☐	Do I need to ask any questions before I begin?
☐	☐	Do I have the materials I need? If not, what do I need?
☐	☐	Have I chosen the best place to work?
☐	☐	Do I have enough space to work? If not, what are my options?
☐	☐	Do I know the time limit?
☐	☐	Do I know what to do when I complete my task?

Figure 5.9   Sample Class Observation Checklist

Student _____

Observation Focus _____ Subject _____

Rated by: Teacher _____ Peer _____ Self _____

Date _____   Class _____

Key: O = Outstanding S = Satisfactory   N = Needs improvement

Student's Name	Skill 1	Skill 2	Skill 3	Skill 4	Comments
1.					
2.					
3.					

Figure 5.10   Sample Oral Report Checklist

Sample Oral Report Checklist

Name _____ Date _____ Topic _____

Evaluate all elements with the following key:

O = Outstanding   S = Satisfactory   N = Needs to Improve

_____ Accuracy of Information
_____ Quality
_____ Quantity
_____ Organization
_____ Structure of material clear to listener
_____ Details to support or elaborate
        sections

_____ Proportionate time, based on relative
        importance of segments
_____ Presentation
_____ Posture
_____ Voice clarity
_____ Energy

Comments

ASSESS READING AND WRITING SKILLS

In every subject it is important to know the student's reading and writing ability level. Success in each content area depends on the learner's skills in understanding passages and in expressing thoughts in written communications. The following assessments provide quick and easy ways to identify the learner's approximate ability level in reading and writing.

Oral Reading Assessment

A quick, informal way to check comprehension ability is to read selected passages to the student. Ask the learner to orally rephrase or summarize the passages using the important ideas. A student who cannot comprehend a passage while reading silently usually has a higher level of understanding when it is read aloud.

Check Oral Reading with questions similar to the following:

1. Name three important facts from your reading.
2. Choose one fact, and tell why it is important.
3. Identify an important event, and tell when it occurred.
4. Where have you heard or used this information?
5. When did this event happen?
6. Why did this event happen?
7. Summarize the information.

If the student has difficulty with oral reading skills, provide time for him or her to practice before requiring oral reading.

Prompts for Writing

Present the students with a prompt for their writing experience. Before they begin writing, share a checklist like the one below. This shows the learners the observable measures of success to check their writing and how to self-assess as they write.

As prompts, choose questions or statements related to a familiar topic.

Examples:

- Write about a favorite time in your life.
- What is the most frightening event you can remember?
- Describe your favorite free-time activity for a friend.
- Describe a character from your favorite book, sitcom, or movie.

Figure 5.11 Reading Comprehension Assessment

Huh?	Need more details	Message is clear	Message glows

Strike out	Double	Triple	Home Run

Writing Sample

Student _____ Date _____

Writing Sample Title _____

Evaluator: _____ Self _____ Teacher _____ Peer _____ Parent

Scoring Scale: + Yes   − No   ? Not Yet

Note: If a student has difficulty writing, draw a smiley face on a sticky note. Place the drawing where it is visible. Instruct the learner to tell every word to the face. This causes the writer to write with organized content. This is beneficial for the student who can tell it but has trouble writing down the information.

Individual Observation Checklist

A checklist form similar to the following may be used whenever a student is working alone. Also, it may be used when it is beneficial to observe and assess the learner during participation in a large or small group activity.

> *Occupy the learner's hands; stimulate his mind!*

Name _____ Date _____

Skill, Standard, or Behavior	Yes	Some	No
1. _____	_____	_____	_____
2. _____	_____	_____	_____
3. _____	_____	_____	_____

Figure 5.12   Assessing a Written Assignment

Content = 60 points

1. _____ Do all the details relate to the same topic?

   Rate
   1 2 3 4   _____ × 15 = _____

2. _____ Are there enough details and examples?

3. _____ Do the writing responses make sense?

4. _____ Are you able to understand the plot or important points?

Organization = 25 points

1. _____ Does the writing have a beginning, middle, and end?

   Rate
   1 2 3   _____ × 8.5 = _____

2. _____ Are the events in order?

3. _____ Are the facts and ideas in the best order for the reader?

Mechanics = 15 points

1. _____ Do mechanical writing errors hinder the reading of the sample?

   Rate
   1 2 3 4 5   _____ × 3 = _____

2. _____ Are most of the words spelled correctly?

3. _____ Are most of the punctuation marks in place?

4. _____ Were most of the capital letters used correctly?

5. _____ Is the writing legible?

Signature _____   Date _____ Total Score = _____ out of 100

Manipulatives

Manipulatives are tangible, concrete forms or objects used in authentic tasks to demonstrate, discover, draw a conclusion, or prove what is known. Hands-on experiences give students opportunities to see and

Figure 5.13 Individual Observation Checklist

Student _____   Date _____

Subject, Situation, or Assignment _____

Observer _____ Teacher _____ Self _____ Peer

Behavior or Task Observed	Frequently	Sometimes	Very Little	Comments
1.				
2.				
3.				

Summary Comments:

Signature of Observer _____   Date _____

touch an object. Some learners need to use manipulatives for an extended period of time. When a student automatically works several problems correctly without the manipulative, he or she is solving it mentally. When this occurs, the student has moved from the concrete, hands-on level of learning to the abstract level.

Sample Manipulatives Assessment

Use the scale in Figure 5.14 to assess the student's concrete-to-abstract level of learning.

Figure 5.14   Sample Manipulatives Assessment

Use the following scale to assess the student's concrete-to-abstract level of learning.

$\longleftarrow$ ──────────────────────────────── $\longrightarrow$

| Often needs and | Occasionally | No use of manipulatives |
| uses manipulatives | uses manipulatives | |

Anecdotal Assessment

Anecdotal assessment consists of brief informal notes that record data to assist or teach the learner. The anecdotal record is the documentation written during observations of a student's work or behavior. For example, a teacher might record the strategies a student uses during independent reading activities.

Recording Anecdotal Notes

1. Write the student's name, time, activity or subject, and date on the top of the note.

2. Record each observation in clear, concise terms.

3. Create a management system that works for you to record observations, such as index cards, self-stick notes, or a log. Each entry needs to record a specific observable behavior.

Examples:

- Clipboard Classnotes (See the Clipboard Classnotes activity in this chapter.)
- Card Cruising (See the Card Cruising activity in this chapter.)

Tips for Anecdotal Note Observations

With specific data, be sure to record the date and time of the observation. Always remember that anything written about a student is public record. Avoid subjective comments and adjectives. Record information, like that in the following list, for later use in assisting the student:

- Level of understanding
- The approach used
- Attitude
- Participation
- Productivity

- Time on task
- Commitment to accomplishing the task
- Concentration
- Ability to cope with particular situations (Record the time, place, and cause of frustration, distraction, or boredom.)
- Ability to work alone, with a partner, or in a small group
- Areas of strength
- Areas of weakness
- Positive behaviors
- Negative behaviors and reactions

During an observation the teacher must be alert to the learner's needs. Successes must be noted and praised. The most valuable notes contain assessment data to analyze what, how, why, and when this student is learning. The information is used to design instruction for the individual.

Clipboard Classnotes

Clipboard Classnotes is a way to organize anecdotal notes while assessing a task, action, demonstration, or event based on specific observable comments. Date the entry and add the time of day. Document positive and negative behaviors as well as evidence of individual strengths and weaknesses. One can see patterns of behaviors, actions, and habits being developed, formed, and learned (see Table 5.1).

Use the following guidelines for assessment using the Clipboard Classnotes strategy:

1. Attach self-stick notes to a clipboard.

2. If particular students are to be observed, place each student's name and date at the top of the self-stick note. This reminds the observer to strategically observe the notable behaviors and actions of the identified students. Add some blank self-stick notes to record observations of unexpected and noteworthy behaviors or skills of other students.

3. Write notes about the specific behaviors observed. Consistent note taking identifies behavior patterns.

Card Cruising

Use one large index card for each student. Punch a hole in the upper left corner of each card, and slide a ring clasp or similar gadget through the hole in the cards to create a quick-flip assessment tool. Write a student's name in the top right-hand corner of the card. Alphabetize the cards by last

Table 5.1   Observation Spots

Use the following chart to note specific areas while observing the total student.

Academic Performance	Behavior
Understandings and misconceptions Following directions Strengths and weaknesses Failures and successes Strong points and weak spots	Attitudes and interests Independence Social interactions Attitudes Positive and negative behaviors
Interest	Thinking Skills
Likes and dislikes Time on task Choices Level of motivation	Critical thinking Creativity Processing techniques Problem-solving ability

names. Add the student's phone number and other important information in the corner space for easy access. Keep them handy to jot down notes from observations.

Assessing With Journals

To avoid having students approach journal activities with dread, build anticipation to creative journal assignments such as a Double Entry Journal or a Partner Journal (see Figures 5.15, 5.16, and 5.17). Instead of thinking "Oh no, not journals again!" your students will clamor for their next chance to try an interesting writing experience. Journals are excellent assessment tools. If a student uses a skill automatically and correctly in a journal activity, it is mastered.

Jazzy Journal Assessment

Jazzy Journals make assessment activities interesting and exciting. Challenge students to add their ideas to create Jazzy Journal entries. Consider these suggestions for journal assessment entries:

- Design a sequence.
- Sketch or draw a picture.
- Create a caricature.
- Use a graphic organizer.
- Make a graffiti list using various fonts and colors.
- Create a song, rap, jingle, rhyme, or cheer.

Use Jazzy Journal entries to process information. When students use their ideas to create metaphors or similes, they remember facts and concepts, because their brains create links or connections.

Example

The (fact, concept, standard, skill) is like _____ because _____.

a musical instrument	a type of music	a particular song
an animal	a piece of clothing	a piece of furniture
a vehicle	a trip	a color
a sport	an event	an experience

Encourage students to "jazz up" their journals by using a combination of one or more of the following:

colored yarn	cutout shapes	drawings
hole-punched dots	miniature sketches	magazine clippings
neon colors	photos	pipe cleaners
ribbons	sayings	scrapbooking pieces
stamps	stars	stickers
symbols	thumbprint drawings	varied fonts
varied line widths		

Figure 5.15 Double Entry Journal Form

Use a form similar to the following to create double entry journal space. Encourage students to personalize these pages with color, designs, and various fonts as time permits.

Name _____   Grade _____

Topic _____   Date _____

A. First Notes Date ____	B. Second Notes Date ____

Figure 5.16   Partner Journals

Partner Journals

Partners A and B write their ideas about the topic or question in the appropriate column. Then they take turns writing to assist each other with deeper understanding as they iron out answers to questions or come up with solutions.

1. Partner A	2. Partner B

Figure 5.17   Note Journal Form

A Note Journal form can be used by students to record important information during various study phases of a specific topic or unit.

What I Know	Notes From First Reading	Notes From Lecture	Notes to Study

Process Journals

The Process Journal allows students to log their thinking while applying information in the procedural steps of an event, experiment, or project (see Figure 5.18).

Learning Log: Assessing an Ongoing Project or Assignment

Use Learning Logs as assessment tools to monitor the learner's progress and work level and check for understanding (see Figure 5.19). At

Figure 5.18   Process Sample Forms

Process Sample Form I

Monday	Tuesday	Wednesday	Thursday	Friday

Process Sample Form II

A	B	C	D	E

Figure 5.19   Learning Log

Learning Log

Student or Group _____

Assignment _____

Day 1. Description of Work Today   Date _____

```
┌──────────────────────────────────────────────────────────────────┐
│                                                                    │
│                                                                    │
│                                                                    │
└──────────────────────────────────────────────────────────────────┘
```

Day 2. Description of Work Today   Date _____

```
┌──────────────────────────────────────────────────────────────────┐
│                                                                    │
│                                                                    │
│                                                                    │
└──────────────────────────────────────────────────────────────────┘
```

Day 3. Description of Work Today   Date _____

```
┌──────────────────────────────────────────────────────────────────┐
│                                                                    │
│                                                                    │
│                                                                    │
└──────────────────────────────────────────────────────────────────┘
```

Note: This continues each day of the assignment.

the conclusion of a unit of study, the logs, like process journals, become a record of a student's learning journey.

Graphic Organizers

Graphic organizers are visual representations used to record information. Facts and ideas are easier to manipulate, process, and remember when they are applied in a visual way. As learners complete a graphic organizer, they actively engage their thinking as the design is completed with words or phrases. This visual representation links information in various ways to create personal connections.

Including graphic organizers on tests would be more creative, challenging, and fun than most traditional objective-style items. (Burke, 1994)

Add novelty to students' experiences with graphic organizers to enhance their memory of information. Most students are familiar with numerous font styles found in word processing programs. Encourage the use of different print styles and sizes for specific subtopics or levels of the assessment tool. For example, record the major topic in a large font with each subtopic in a smaller font. Decreasing various font sizes emphasizes the decreasing value of each subtopic level. Graphic organizers empower learners with realistic assessment tools for meaningful learning experiences (see Figure 5.20).

For example, write on the hand organizer five things to remember about a topic, standard, concept, character, or reading selection.

Prompts for Assessment

Prompts activate thinking about a specific topic or term. Use the following assessment prompts:

- The most fabulous fact I learned today is _____.
- The most interesting fact I learned today is _____.
- In our last lesson, I remember _____.
- I want to learn about _____.
- My learning goal for this topic of study is _____.
- I do not understand _____.

Figure 5.20 PMI Charts

Pluses, "+" I like I know I agree I can use	Minuses, "–" I do not like I do not know I disagree with I cannot use	Intriguing I am still thinking about . . . This reminded me that . . . Suggestions I want to know more about . . .

Variation: PMIS	Pluses	Minuses	Intriguing	Suggestions

Wondering Wizard: Performance Assessment

The teacher becomes a Wondering Wizard whenever it is important to unveil a learner's thinking. Discuss the wonders of the brain and the fact that every mind solves problems in different ways. Teachers are like wizards because they know how, when, and where to present quality choices that match the learning. This gives students opportunities to show what they know in their creative ways through performance assessment opportunities.

Give an Example	Explain	Demonstrate	Act It Out	Role-Play
Create a skit	Create a simulation	Show it	Draw it	Illustrate it
Analyze it	Put it to a beat	Create it	Tell it	Use a manipulative
Show me	Take it apart	Put it back together	Tell about it	
Design it	Create it	Contrast it	Compare it	Compact it
Plot it	Make it smaller	Chart it	Write it on a chart	Develop scenes of character's actions
Apply it in another situation	Place it on a spot	Make a timeline	Write from character's point of view	
Make a bar graph	Make a line graph	Create a pie chart	Make a puppet	
Design a cartoon	Create a character and dress it	Create a diorama		
Make a display about the character	Design a book about the character	Display it		
Design a play	Plot on a graphic organizer			
Create a brochure	Design a bulletin board			

Teacher-Made Tests

The most effective tests are made by the teacher for a specific individual or a particular group of students. The same test should not be used with all classes. Standards and units change, and information varies, so do not use the same tests year after year. Students also change. Assessments that guide instruction must change accordingly. Customize plans for instruction for the current needs of individuals or the group.

Quality, effective tests are developed by the teacher who provides instruction for the skill or unit. This individual knows the students better than anyone else and is familiar with instruction students have received and the materials and resources used. Teacher-made tests provide opportunities to differentiate assessment with tools and strategies that are thoughtfully tailored for the learners.

What Does an Effective Teacher-Made Test Show?

Teacher-made tests reveal the following:

- The student's strengths and needs
- The skills or concepts the learner needs to learn next
- Misconceptions that require reteaching or more background
- How the student is processing information
- The learner's interpretations

Use a Checklist to Analyze the Value of the Teacher-Made Test

- Does the test show what the student knows?
- Is the testing format holding the student back from revealing his or her knowledge?
- Format examples: performance, demonstration, written, list, graphic organizer
- When is the most effective time for this test?
- Can it be used as a pretest and a posttest?
- Is it best used during the teaching of the unit for measuring needs and progress?
- Is it better to use this assessment at the end as a summative evaluation of the information learned?
- Why is the information being tested?
- Does the student really need to know this information or skill as a key link or step for past or future learning?
- Is this information needed for lifelong learning?
- Has the student demonstrated that he or she knows the information in other ways, such as telling or in a demonstration?

- What types of question formats are needed for this learner?
- Is appropriate time allowed for taking the test with these questions?
- Is each question clearly stated so the student understands the desired answer?
- Is there enough information given so the student can work independently?
- How will the test be scored or graded?
- Do some sections of the instrument need to be worth more points than other sections?

Format Options for Teacher-Made Tests

Students learn how to follow a variety of directions when they are presented with a variety of assessment formats. Explain how to approach each of the following testing formats when they are introduced. Periodically review the procedures. Model your thinking for each approach by verbalizing your thoughts, or self-talk. This shows students how to use their metacognitive skills. Also, lead conversations and share tips that show students how to work with the various assessment forms.

True/False. Remember, students have a 50 percent chance of getting these questions right or wrong. Guessing plays a vital role in addressing this assessment format. True/false questions are easy to grade.

Multiple-Choice. Teach students each of the following strategies to approach and process multiple-choice problems.

1. It is usually easy to narrow the responses to two possible, correct answers.
   a. Explain *why* the least obvious answers do not work.
   b. Explain why a response is easy to eliminate as an *incorrect* answer.

2. Select the correct answer.

3. Students explain why the remaining responses almost tricked them. Identify the key words or phrases.

Fill in the Blank. Students recall facts and details from the studied information and record their answers. The following are examples of fill-in-the-blank, short answer questions:

1. The definition of the word *hibernation* is _____.

2. The _____, _____, and _____ are the three branches of government.

Open-Ended. Open-ended questions or statements give students opportunities to respond in details in their own words. These are often called discussion questions.

- *Explain* the steps in a long division problem.
- How do cells *divide?*

Performance Tests. A performance test involves the student in hands-on experiences or demonstrations that are designed to show the student's ability and prove understanding. This can be a lab experiment or a simulation. It may involve an ongoing activity to show what the student knows, or it may conclude with a onetime performance. For example, the student may show where Egypt is located on the map or move the hands on a clock so the time shown is one o'clock. He or she may use manipulatives to demonstrate a solution to a problem. Refer to the Wondering Wizard chart in this chapter for a hodgepodge of performance assessment ideas.

Skills Test. A skills test gives the student an opportunity to perform skills in a demonstration. Examples of skills tests include making a birdhouse in the woodworking shop, serving a volleyball in physical education, or applying a specific computer skill in a program.

Problem-Based Model. The problem-based model uses a real-life situation or problem and produces reports, artifacts, and collections as data. The problem, essential question, or hypothesis is often chosen to investigate a local, state, national, or global problem that interests students.

Assessing With a Blank Page

Often teachers hear a student say, "I studied so hard for this test, but I studied all the wrong things!" The student feels the time was wasted because the responses did not demonstrate what was truly learned about the new topic. To eliminate this problem, add a blank page to the test, and give the student an opportunity to write what he or she knows about the topic.

This novel idea helps the teacher learn information the student knows. Do not remove points if the test-taker does not add to the blank page. Give extra points when the student correctly extends a response or states information not addressed on the test. Consider giving the student one point for each piece of content information added to the test. It must be information not included on the test. If the student adds 10 facts or ideas to an already perfect score, the score becomes 110 points.

Provide the blank-page assessment as an option, not as a mandate. Give praise or extra points for accurate responses. This is an exciting way for students to show what they know. This motivates students to study and prepare for assessment.

Assessing with a prompt challenges students to write a note or letter to the teacher when an assessment activity is completed. Use the following prompts as needed:

I learned that	I was surprised that	I discovered that
I still do not understand	I was disappointed that	Next time I hope we
I will remember	The easiest part was	The best part was
I was pleased that	The hardest part was	The most challenging
An interesting part was	I am still thinking about	part was
I needed someone	I believe that	I am sure about
I wonder if	One solution is	To explain
This reminds me of	I can apply this	I predict that

Portfolios

The word *portfolio* is derived from the Latin words *portare*, which means "to carry," and *foglio*, which refers to "a leaf or sheet of paper." The term portfolio is common in the art and business world, where it refers to a case that holds artwork, sheets of paper, official documents, or artifacts. In the classroom, teachers and students use portfolios of various sizes, shapes, and forms to collect and organize work samples. The teacher guides the students as they individually assume responsibility for completing and gathering samples of their work and other entries for their portfolios.

Portfolio Assessment

In portfolio assessment the students, teachers, and parents monitor progress through collected work samples. The major purpose of portfolio assessment is to engage students in the evaluation and identification of their needs and strengths and to show growth and progress.

The needs and strengths of students can be identified in their individual portfolio collections. This information provides assessment data to evaluate and guide their instruction. Analysis of a student's work samples provides data that reflects understanding of a particular standard or skill. The teacher uses the information to identify gaps in learning so the student receives the instruction he or she needs to learn next. The information derived through portfolio assessment becomes a vital tool to guide instructional planning.

Portfolio assessment is designed to do the following:

- Empower learners
- Show stages of progress and performance
- Increase the student's responsibility in learning
- Improve self-efficacy, the *"I can do"* feeling
- Teach students to be self-reflective
- Provide avenues for self-analysis and self-improvement
- Guide students to higher levels of thinking through self-evaluation and peer critique
- Generate genuine pride in accomplishments
- Create a Showcase for Success
- Support grades
- Reveal needs and strengths
- Show evidence of the learner's ability

What Can Be Used as a Portfolio?

Keep in mind that the major purpose of the portfolio is to gather work samples that reflect the student's best work and needs. If a portfolio assessment activity is planned more than one time during the year, vary the collection tools, the collection process, and the presentation style. Adapt the examples in Table 5.2 to create novel portfolio assessment experiences.

Table 5.2   Portfolio Options

Collection Devices	Cover Designs	Page Layout	Gathering Process	Presentation Style
• Folder • Case • Crate • Notebook • Box • X-ray folder • Large envelope • Poster board (folded or stapled) • Web site • CD-ROM	• Graffiti • Geometric shapes • Topic symbols • Scrapbook ideas • Photos • Drawings • Home page	• Frames • Collages • Illustrations • Examples • Scrapbooking ideas • Transparency sleeve • Pictures	• 3–4 examples • Selected passages • Highlights • Summaries • Showcase • Display or exhibit • Web • Interview • Research • Independent practice • Photos	• Oral report • Interview • Conference • Conversation • Circles • Family night • Slide presentation with narration • Talk show • Documentary • Booklet • Diary • Journal

Portfolio Briefs

The word *brief* is derived from the Latin word *breve*, which means "summary." When the term *brief* refers to important documents, it means "a condensed version that includes major facts or points."

A shorter version of the traditional portfolio, a portfolio brief, adds novelty to assignments. The portfolio brief contains student-selected highlights from work samples. In other words, it is a sample of a sample. Each entry contains a succinct or concise view of a student's strengths and needs. This work collection technique has advantages over the traditional portfolio because the amount of time needed for data analysis is greatly reduced. A large amount of time that the teacher and the student usually spend sifting through numerous, detailed activities and work samples is eliminated.

The teacher and students may need to develop new mind-sets to create portfolio briefs. In a traditional portfolio, students place numerous pages that reflect their abilities. The portfolio brief challenges the student to select samples as highlights of the best work. Each entry in the portfolio becomes a snapshot of the learner's ability. The selection process teaches students to assess their daily work and leads to self-directed learning.

My best work is _____.

I need help with _____.

Sample assignments for Portfolio Brief entries:

Writing

- Choose the best paragraph from your essay, and paste it at the top of a piece of paper. Rate your work on a scale from 2 through 10. Write two sentences describing how to improve your work.
- In 25 to 30 words, describe the most important person or event in our lesson today.
- List five important facts from today's lesson.
- Write a word problem that illustrates the math procedure we learned today.
- Complete the last five problems.
- Retell the information through a conversation between two thumbprint or stick characters.
- Retell the passage and write it in your own words. Create a design using one or more symbols repeatedly around the writing to create a frame.
- What will happen next? Draw stick figures with speech bubbles to illustrate your thoughts.

Create a Brief-Preparation Center. Adapt the following center ideas for your students:

- Materials: scissors, hole punch, stapler with staples, highlighter, markers, glue, glitter pens, wallpaper scraps, stickers, construction paper scraps, and paper in various colors and designs. Use materials in neon colors whenever available.

Showcase Scoring

Students and teachers develop a scoring rubric for the portfolio assessment.

5. *Above and Beyond*
   - Completed more activities than those required
   - All assignments are complete and organized
   - Turned everything in on time

4. *On Track*
   - All assignments are complete
   - The work is organized
   - Completed on time

3. *Not Quite There*
   - Missing one or two pieces
   - Not well organized
   - One day late

2. *Thrown Together*
   - Three or more pieces missing
   - Organization
   - Two days late

1. *A "No Show" Effort*
   - Did not try
   - No examples of ability
   - More than two days late

Select appropriate assessment tools to use at the end of the learning to discover the student's insights, progress with skills, and knowledge level. The data represent what the learner knows at this point in time. The information guides planning for the next unit or topic of study.

Give students opportunities to apply the mastered skills in new ways for practice and review. Teach the skills that are not mastered in new ways by planning customized approaches to incorporate the learners' intelligences and learning styles. Share the results and plans with the students.

Teach students the value of ipsative assessment. This is a form of continuous monitoring for self-improvement. For example, when someone begins an exercise program, ipsative assessment is evident when the individual says, "The last time I did this exercise, I could complete ten sets. Today I completed seven sets. The next time I need to . . . ." He may say, "I improved so much today, I need to continue these approaches and add . . . ." Self-directed learners routinely apply ipsative assessment in their daily activities. Design your plans to teach the valuable skills needed for students to learn self-assessment strategies they can use in their academic and personal activities.

As a unit of study or lesson segment comes to conclusion, identify the strategies and activities that made your learners successful. Abandon the techniques that did not work for you. Explore new ways to meet your learners' needs. This approach presents assessment as a continuous learning adventure that creates new discoveries for you and your students.

Assessing 6
Learning in
Differentiated
Instructional
Models and
Strategies

Essential Question: How can we incorporate strong differentiated assessments within the models and strategies that are frequently used to differentiate instruction?

A major goal of differentiated assessment is to diagnose learners in different ways. The activities embedded in learning models provide a varied selection of assessment strategies. Adapt the tips, techniques, and suggestions to your student's assessment needs.

The models discussed in this chapter are the Curriculum Compacting Model, the Contract Model, the Project Model, and the Problem-Based Model. The Adjustable Assignment Model is discussed in Chapter 8 because it is an effective planning tool to adjust assignments so they meet the learner's needs.

The instructional strategies examined in this chapter include cubing, choice boards, and agendas. Ideas are presented for establishing centers, labs, and stations. Flexible grouping scenarios and designs are explored for effective planning and assessment.

◆

CURRICULUM COMPACTING MODEL

The Curriculum Compacting Model is used when a teacher realizes that the student knows the upcoming material. A customized instructional plan is designed to extend or enrich learning experiences. This permits the student to skip portions of the curriculum that he or she knows (Reis & Purcell, 1993). This model presents a different way for the student to work with the information.

Use a variety of work samples and preassessments to identify the student who does not need to sit through the next instructional teaching segment. If the student has demonstrated that he or she already knows the information and can apply the learning elsewhere, the student is ready for this independent activity. If the activities are boring, the student may be nonproductive, and the time will have been wasted! The Curriculum Compacting Model gives the learner opportunities to increase his or her knowledge base and excel.

The following scenario illustrates the importance of differentiated instruction. A teacher felt that one student in math class knew so much about the lessons that the student could have taught the prealgebra class. Out of boredom, the student exhibited inappropriate behaviors and an "I don't care" attitude. This behavior affected his performance and the performance of his classmates. The student was moved from a prealgebra class to a high school Algebra I class. After one week of leaving the middle school and joining the Algebra I class, the student's attitude and performance in all academic subjects improved because this student was academically challenged and successful. A curriculum compacting assignment is carried out at a specific time to meet the needs of the student and teacher.

Ways to Use Curriculum Compacting

The Curriculum Compacting Model was originally designed for students who needed a form of accelerated learning. In the following adaptations of the model, it is used with students who need foundation knowledge and experiences before they are introduced to the current lesson.

Working With the Novice

If assessment data reveals that students do not have the appropriate background and skills to learn the information, their needs may be met by a curriculum compacting assignment. Results of an informal or formal preassessment identify the "gaps in the learning" or the skills and information a student needs to learn next. The teacher decides the best way to provide experiences on a student's readiness level.

Working With the Expert

When assessment reveals that a student knows the material and can apply, interpret, and adapt the information to real-life situations, the Curriculum Compacting Model can be used to plan activities that interest the student and motivate him or her to learn more about the topic or concept. This student has an extensive knowledge base and is ready to learn more and to dig deeper into the topic. The student is ready to move on to a new concept, skill, or subtopic. Offer the student choices related to the topic, send him or her to another teacher's class to be challenged, or design a contract with the student that requires the use of higher-order thinking skills or more challenging materials. This method avoids placing a cap on an individual's potential.

Compacting Scenarios

Individual Students

- Tasks are selected, adjusted, and paced to meet the student's needs.
- The student goes to another room to be challenged.
- A tutor works with the student.
- The student and teacher design a contract.

Total Grade-Level Compacting

The following compacting model is designed for a class with a diverse knowledge base related to a unit:

1. Designate one teacher as the focus teacher.

2. Target a topic of weakness.

3. Give a pretest of the skills to all students.

4. Record scores from high to low.

5. Select the students with the top 20 scores in the classroom to work with the focus teacher during the period dedicated to the topic.

6. The focus teacher keeps the students in his or her class whose scores fell among the top 20. The remaining students are dispersed heterogeneously among the other grade-level teachers for the unit or topic of study.

7. Students go to their designated classes each day during the focus period.

8. Give a posttest to assess individual progress and needs.

Using a strong preassessment activity, identify students who need more assistance in learning a particular skill or subject. These students may lack prior experience and basic knowledge to work on this skill, standard, or objective. Provide them with opportunities to work on the fundamentals required for a specific topic or skill on their grade level. They must be brought up to the readiness level for the new information so it becomes possible for effective learning to occur.

Often teachers do not feel responsible for basic information or skills that students did not master in the previous grade. Teachers have so many standards to teach in the subject areas for their grade levels that there is no time to go back and reteach to meet the needs of these students. When it is obvious that students cannot move to new learning without the basics or prior knowledge, a way must be found to provide the foundation they need. All students must be prepared to learn!

CONTRACT MODEL

Student Contract Request Form

A contract is a work agreement between a teacher and a student that facilitates differentiated instruction. If the student is capable, he or she fills out the contract form, requesting permission to work with the information in his or her own way or to complete a specific project. Develop the form with a timeline and the student's plan mapped out for discussion and approval before the work begins. It is important that the teacher and learner understand each part of the contract. The contract is submitted for the teacher's approval and signature.

A Contract That Works

Differentiating assessments with contracts assures student accountability in the following ways:

- The teacher and student develop a list of tasks and activities to be completed with specific requirements.
- The student completes the contract within a specific time frame.
- Tasks and activities are adjusted to the student's readiness level and interests.
- The pace of instruction and practice time are modified.

- The contract appropriately fits the purpose and the student.
- The activities teach students the concepts or skills needed for their age and grade level.

Assess the Value and Usefulness of the Contract

The following checklist is designed for a teacher to analyze a contract and determine its usefulness. It is an effective way for the student to work according to his or her individual needs and the assessed standards. Design a form similar to the following to assess the contract's value and usefulness:

The contract meets the following requirements:

☐ Outlines the content at the student's level to be assessed at this time

☐ Adds worthwhile information or skills to this student's knowledge base

☐ Meets the needed objectives

☐ Meets the established timeline

☐ Uses the student's time wisely

☐ Helps the student learn how to apply time-management techniques

☐ Allows for individual choices and interests

☐ Challenges the student's mind

☐ Can be completed with little adult supervision

☐ Honors the student's unique strengths, talents, and interests

☐ Engages a student with a sense of personal ownership

☐ Encourages creativity

☐ Develops problem-solving and thinking skills

☐ Provides productive learning experiences

Comments

Remember! A contract is effective when the assignment challenges the student's mind and expands this knowledge base. The tasks must be focused so the learner can work independently with minimal assistance from the teacher. Contracts should only be assigned when they provide worthwhile experiences. Avoid "contractitis."

PROJECT-BASED MODEL

A Project-Based model fosters expanded independent study on a specific topic. This model can be designed as a class project, a content-centered project, or a student-choice contract.

Before assigning a project, check to see that it is age-appropriate and that the student will be able to process the information. Design the assignment so the student is challenged but can complete each component independently. In other words, the project must be a student-centered activity, not something that an adult needs to assist or supervise directly. The teacher monitors progress with a process journal or other tool and provides feedback and suggestions along the way.

Relate the assignment to information or skills the student must learn at that grade level or in that content area. Ask the following questions: (a) Will the project meet the student's needs? (b) Is the project a wise use of the student's time? (c) Do the activities enhance the student's understanding of one or more curriculum standards?

Assess the Project-Based Model Assignment

Select the appropriate standard, objective, or benchmark for the content information and grade level. Use the following questions to assess the appropriateness of the project-based assignment before it is presented to the student. If "no" is a response to one or two questions, examine the value of the assignment. If three or more responses are "no," abandon the assignment and replace it with another project that meets the criteria. If all responses are "yes," the assignment is a valuable learning experience.

Preassessing a Project: A Teacher's Checklist

The project-based assignment is . . .	Yes	No
1. Developed with ongoing assessment throughout the work	☐	☐
2. Designed within the student's level of success	☐	☐
3. Content related	☐	☐
4. Designed to be completed independently	☐	☐
5. Devised to engage the student in researching and processing information	☐	☐
6. Designed to fit the time frame	☐	☐
7. Gave the student experience with new learning	☐	☐
8. Filled with high-interest activities	☐	☐
9. Created with accessible resources and materials	☐	☐
10. Designed with progress checkpoints	☐	☐
11. Easily assessed with a rubric	☐	☐

The questions for the teacher and the student assess the feasibility of the project during the selection process. Too often when a teacher gives a student a choice, the choice is made too quickly, without thinking through the process. When this happens, an adult must intervene and assist the learner in the selection process. The student becomes frustrated when the topic is boring, the tasks are too difficult, or appropriate materials are not available. Lead the student through the self-check assessment the first time he or she uses it. The goal of this activity is to show the learner how to carefully analyze a project before it is selected.

Preassessing a Project: A Student's Questionnaire

The student completes a preassessment questionnaire with approximately 10 items. Use questions similar to the following for the learner to analyze interests, abilities, and needs related to the selected project:

- What are the most interesting subtopics of this study for me?
- Which part would make a good project?
- What do I want to learn?
- What is the timeline?
- Will I be able to meet the requirements of the progress checkpoints along the way?
- Where can I find the material and resources?
- What are my greatest concerns or needs?
- What are my main concerns about the assignment?
- What do I need before I begin the project?
- Who do I want to be my peer evaluator or adviser?
- How will the product look when it is finished?
- How will I present the project?
- What are the self-assessment tools I need to use?
- How will my work be assessed?

Assessing a Postproject Display

For the Teacher

When the project is completed, the teacher assesses the value of the displayed learning by using questions similar to the following:

- Did the project tasks address the content objectives and standards?
- Did the student grow in his or her knowledge base through these experiences?
- Are all parts of the project accurate?
- Does the project reflect learning over a period of time?
- Is the student able to explain the information learned?

- Will there be allotted time for students to present the projects?
- Would this project be beneficial for another student?

For the Student

When the student completes a project, he or she assesses the value of the work using reflective prompts similar to the following:

- Was this learning experience worth the time I spent on it? Why or why not?
- I learned . . .
- Where did I need more direction?
- I am proud of the following tasks . . .
- Which tasks did I need more time to complete?
- My deepest thinking was used when . . .
- I want to know more about . . .
- If I could select another project, it would be . . .

PROBLEM-BASED MODEL

The problem-based model makes learning more meaningful and applicable to the real world. Select problems that intrigue and engage learners. Topics may be related to environmental issues, health problems, abuse, taxation, global warming, or other local and national concerns. Usually only one question or problem is developed and posed to the class. Whenever appropriate, differentiate by providing opportunities for students to select the problem. Ask for their suggestions and input about the processes and procedures they will use to solve the problem or essential question. Learners become proactive detectives, investigators, scientists, or inventors when they play a role in the decision-making process.

Examples

How can traffic flow be improved at the intersection near the recreation center?

What can be done to prevent littering on the grounds of our school?

Guidelines for Choosing the Problem: A Student's Questionnaire

The following questionnaire is designed to guide the thinking processes of individuals or small groups in selecting a problem for their work:

- What problem do I want to investigate?
- Will the results make a difference?
- What information and research are needed?
- What steps do I need to take to gather the needed information?
- What materials and resources are needed?
- How will the results be compiled?
- What procedures are needed to solve the problem?
- What checkpoint or self-assessment tool will be used?
- How will the teacher assess my work?
- How will I present the information and my solutions?

Assessing the Problem Choice: A Teacher's Questionnaire

- Is the problem worth the time?
- Do the assignment and activities enhance the content and standards required at this grade level?
- Is it age appropriate?
- Will the results be observable for the learners?
- Are materials and resources accessible?
- How will individual roles and tasks be assigned?
- What checkpoints and self-assessment tools will be used?
- How will I assess the individuals or groups?
- Do the learners understand the assessment process that will be used?

CUBING

Cubing activities are designed to offer students assessment choices and to add novelty to thinking. Create cubes by covering boxes, pieces of foam, or cube-shaped containers.

1. Choose words from the domain of thinking on Bloom's Taxonomy and place one term in each section on the cube (see Figure 6.1). Customize the terms to assess the student on his or her level of thinking.

2. The student selects a side of the cube to complete by rolling the cube or dice, drawing a number, spinning a spinner, or selecting a favorite way to respond.

Variations for Assessment Cubing Activities

- Select six terms from a particular domain that fit the concept, topic, vocabulary word, or artifact in a topic of study.
- Choose an object, and use each term on the cube to describe it. This can be a written or oral activity, depending on the student's needs.

Figure 6.1   Cubing Example

1. Propose	4. Demonstrate
2. Rate	5. Describe
3. Predict	6. Define

- Collectively choose one object to discuss with each of the selected cubing terms.
- Use cubing activities in a center. Students draw or write about a topic, vocabulary word, or concept using the terms.
- Roll a die, and use the term on the cube with the matching number to apply to the object. If two students roll the same number, they apply the word in different ways to describe the object, word, or concept.
- Design cubes with a different assessment activity about a specific topic on each side. The learner rolls the cube to select the task.

CHOICE BOARDS

Choice boards are created with grids that vary in size according to students' needs. Each section of the grid contains an assessment activity. The teacher assigns the activities by offering learners many choices in selecting the sections they complete.

Choice develops confidence, fosters independence, creates a sense of responsibility, and gives students ownership in learning. Eric Jensen (1995), an expert on brain research, refers to choices as key motivators. Jensen emphasizes the teacher's role in finding ways to reach the unmotivated learner. Choice boards motivate students because they provide opportunities for students to choose their assessment activities. They give teachers flexible tools to create assessment assignments for all subject areas and skills. Each activity on the choice board is specifically designed to assess a standard, skill, or concept and meet students' varied needs, abilities, and interests.

Designing Choice Boards

Prior to designing a choice board, consider how much experience students have in making choices. If students have had few or no opportunities to make selection decisions, begin with the smaller four-square or tic-tac-toe design.

Examples

- Use a four-square outline to create four choices.
- Use a tic-tac-toe outline to create nine choices.
- Use a bingo board outline to create 25 choices.

Adding Novelty

To add novelty to choice boards, use topic or seasonal shapes, outlines, or unique designs as the background on which to place the choice board selections. Try some of these suggestions or create your own!

Suggested outlines:

- Wheel
- Hand shape
- Pizza
- Rainbow
- Flower petals
- Rocket
- Pyramid
- Flags

One of the most effective choice boards is designed to match the number of quality assessment activities brainstormed by the students. Use the following guidelines to design quality choice boards for assessment experiences:

1. Select a place in the lesson plans where the criteria and the assessments lend themselves to a choice board.

2. Brainstorm an extensive list of assessment choice activities. Give students opportunities to brainstorm the activities, too. This is an enticing way for students to learn many self-assessment strategies and practice using them.

3. Place a check mark beside activities on the list that meet the student's assessment needs for the learning standard.

4. Count the number of check marks.

5. Place each chosen assessment activity on a large index card.

6. Draw a choice board grid using a shape to fit the number of selected activities.

7. Place each selected card on a section of the choice board.

8. Number each choice.

Variation: If a grid is used, and there are an odd number of choices, place a wild card in the center as an option. When the wild card space is selected, the student creates an assessment tool or strategy.

Using Choice Boards Wisely

Choice boards are flexible assessment tools. The following list contains various ways to present the tasks:

- Base the assignment on the winning strategy for a tic-tac-toe or bingo game.
  - ▲ For example, complete a horizontal, vertical, or diagonal row of activities.
- Place assessment activities for the novice learner in the even-numbered sections.
- Use the odd-numbered sections for assessment activities designed to challenge students with a high degree of mastery.
- Create assignments that give students opportunities to use a random selection process.
  - ▲ For example, select three activities from the choice board to complete.
- Assign specific items that meet the learner's needs.
  - ▲ Consider the following examples:
    - ▪ Complete the bottom row of assessment activities on the choice board.
    - ▪ Complete the activities in the four corners.
- Place a letter (e.g., *A, B, C, D* . . .) above each column, and number the rows (i.e., 1, 2, 3, 4 . . .). Strategically place specific assessment activities to accommodate individual or group needs.
  - ▲ For example, complete A4, C2, D3, and an activity of your choice.
- Use a crucial skill in the wild card space, and make it a requirement for the assignment.
  - ▲ Consider the following examples:
    - ▪ Everyone must complete a row that includes the center box.
    - ▪ Complete the activity in the center space and two activities of your choice.

Note: Give the student opportunities to design and select the choice board activities whenever possible.

Figure 6.2   Assessment Choice Board

Use an Idea Tree to show the causes and effects of _____.	Plot the information you learned about your favorite character on a stick figure.	Compare and contrast the two events on a Venn diagram.
Use a Concept Map to organize the important details of the study.	Design a sequence chart for important events in the study.	Place five important facts on a Hand Organizer.

Liz Bennett, an educational consultant and trainer, reminds teachers to avoid giving choices at the expense of learning. Students naturally make choices that match their strongest learning styles, intelligences, and interests. When choices are given in all situations, "their strengths become stronger, and their weaknesses become weaker." Teachers should use their knowledge of students and sound planning strategies to decide when choice assessment activities are valuable experiences.

Figure 6.2 presents innovative ways for students to show what they have learned from a text passage, a specific reading selection, a unit, or a subject. Students may be given a rubric or checklist for the assessment activities so they know the criteria and descriptors of success.

Challenge students by giving them opportunities to design assessment strategies and tools for the choice board. When students know how to create assessment activities, they can apply this strategy as a self-assessment tool during independent work.

The self-selection process gives learners a voice in the assessment process. Students enjoy choosing the activities that allow them to apply information in different ways to show what they know.

AGENDAS

Agendas are specific assignments strategically planned to meet the needs of an individual or a small group. Agendas are occasionally referred to as menus. They are implemented to manage independent work time when individual students need experiences with different skills, topics, concepts, interests, information, or strategies. Students work with their personal agendas while other members of the group work on a different lesson or activity.

The teacher explains the list of activities in the agenda assignment and sets the deadline. The agenda includes several opportunities for student choice, such as selection of activities, the order of completion, or the pacing for each item on the agenda. The assignments are placed in a folder,

Figure 6.3   Agenda Assignment Sample

Student _____   Date _____

❑ Read pages _____, and take notes in a unique way.

❑ Make a collage about what you learned from the _____.

❑ Complete the computer program ____.

❑ Choose two activities to complete from the choice board.

    Due _____

    Student's Signature _____

    Teacher's Signature _____

    Reflections

chart, or specified section of the room (see Figure 6.3). Because the student has detailed, outlined assignments and tasks designed for his or her readiness level, the student is able to work independently.

When agenda items are checked or routinely assessed, a log of the student's work is created. As learners engage in regular assessments, they become aware of their needs, rates of progress, and successes.

Assess the Agenda Plan

Use the following questions to assess the agenda plan.

Does this agenda allow the student to do the following:

1. Work with the needed standard and content

2. Learn this information

3. Feel challenged

4. Work at an appropriate pace

5. Choose his or her favorite order for working with the tasks

6. Develop independence

7. Manage personal time

8. Work at his or her readiness level

9. Include a reflection activity

CENTERS, LABS, AND STATIONS FOR ASSESSMENT

Use a variety of centers, labs, or stations for quality-focused assessments that provide challenges with manipulatives. The best time to assess the learner's ability and knowledge is when the individual is actively engaged at his or her own pace.

Exploratory Centers

An Exploratory Center is an excellent place to assess students' performance experiences. Provide materials and set the rules. Students use the materials to discover, invent, create, and process any way they choose. Assess by asking appropriate questions to analyze their thinking process, to explain actions, and to interpret how or why something happened. Use the responses to determine what needs to happen next for students. Design Exploratory Centers to investigate topics in subject areas.

Adapt the following guidelines and rules for an Exploratory Center:

- Use the materials provided.
- Work in the appropriate space.
- Respect others.
- Use materials wisely.
- Display the product in the designated area.
- Organize and clean the work area before leaving it.

Assessment for Exploratory Centers

- The learner stayed on task.
- This center is a wise use of time.
- These activities promote thinking and investigation.
- Materials are appropriate, available, and accessible.
- The mind of the participant is challenged in a novel way.

Structured Centers

Structured Centers may be designed for a specific topic or skill in any subject. The tasks and procedures are established for students to follow. The appropriate materials are available, and the rules are set. Adapt the following guidelines to outline tasks, to present rules, and to select materials for Structured Centers.

Example of a Structured Center Assignment

1. Create a model to teach the information you learned.

2. Place the model on a piece of construction paper.

3. Write your name on or near the model in a visible space.

4. Display your work on the table provided.

Rules

- Use the materials provided.
- Follow and complete the directions.
- Work in the appropriate space.
- Clean up the center and work area before you leave.

Assess the Structured Center

When setting up and implementing a Structured Center, assess it with the following checklist:

____ Objectives and goals are identified.

____ Directions and procedures are clear and concise.

____ Tasks are clearly defined.

____ Activities can be completed without supervision.

____ Materials are available and accessible.

____ Time is used wisely.

Center Management Tips

Some centers are assigned by the teacher. Whenever possible, provide opportunities for students to choose where they will work. A student may work alone, with a partner, or in a small group.

Create signs and labels so students know the location of materials or workstations. If the classroom is not conducive to movement, permit students to create a special work space around their desks. Remember, quality centers can be created with plastic bags, folders, or boxes. Post the center name, rules, directions, and procedures in a visible space with the materials.

Centers are not intended for busywork or for time wasting. If a center is not working or the students are not following the rules, close the center. Keep the center open when it is a productive place. It is fun and useful to design open and closed signs for temporary openings and closings of centers.

Examples

Closed for Repair	Open for Business
Site Under Reconstruction	Grand Opening

Assessing Center Time

The most productive aspect of center time assessment is its ability to provide data on how students process what they are doing, to show how students interpret what they are thinking, and to identify weaknesses and strengths in specific areas. The purpose for assessing center, lab, or workstation time is to record key observations that provide insights into what the student knows. Record and interpret the assessment, then plan for further instruction.

Sample Questioning for Center Time

- Tell me.
- How did you _____?
- Tell me about this.
- Why did you use _____?

Note: See the open-ended questioning section in Chapter 5 for more examples.

ASSESSMENT FOR FLEXIBLE GROUPING

Flexible grouping strategies accommodate the needs of learners for instruction or assessment. The acronym TAPS represents the four basic ways to design assessment groups for learners:

T = Total Group   **A** = Alone   **P** = Partner   **S** = Small Group

Total Group	The entire class is assessed as work is completed, using the same directions and expectations set for everyone.
Alone	Each student works independently on a specific assessment task.
Partners	Two students are assessed as they work together on an open-ended question, a brainstorming activity, a discussion topic, a project, or a presentation.
Small Groups	Four to six students work on an assessment task. Each group member is accountable for his or her own learning. Strengths and talents of individual students shine during challenging cooperative assignments and interesting discussion as students learn from each other.

Grouping Decisions

When grouping students, the teacher decides if it is best for the student to work independently, with a partner, in a small group, or with the total group. The following questionnaire is designed to assist a teacher in assessing optimum grouping designs for use before the teaching, during the learning, and after the experience. Consider the advantages and disadvantages of each grouping design. Analyze responses to determine how the strategy is working. Remember to use flexible grouping to meet specific student needs.

T for Total Group

Assessing Before Teaching

- What parts of the lesson do I need to teach to the total class?
- What is the overall state of readiness for this material and these concepts for this class?
- Are appropriate visuals, props, graphics, and other materials available?
- How will these total-group activities be assessed, informally and formally?

Assessing During the Learning

- Are students learning the appropriate standards, skills, or content?
- Are students involved?
- Are students attentive and listening?
- Do the students show a positive attitude?
- Are the students engaged in applying the information?
- Are learners retaining the information?
- Am I revamping and readjusting my plans to meet the diverse needs of my students?
- Is the time being used productively?

Assessing After the Total Group Experience

- Did the students' responses show that they were learning?
- Did the props, visuals, and materials enhance learning?
- Did the teaching and learning meet the goals and expectations?
- What do the students need next?

Total Group

Advantages	Disadvantages
Directions same for all	Difficult to manage
Teacher directed	Easy for students to get off task
Time saved	Difficult to differentiate
Students hear others' comments	Low level of individual participation

---

A for Alone

Assessing Before Teaching

- What are the specific gaps to be zapped according to the preassessment?
- On which parts do students need to work alone?
- Do I need to set up a choice board?
- Do some students need individual agendas?
- What do I need to teach next?
- Which parts do students need to practice alone?
- How will each experience be assessed?
- What accommodations need to be planned for the low- and high-end learners?

Assessing During the Learning

- Is each student being challenged by the assignment?
- Is each student staying on task?
- How is the student showing his or her understanding?

Assessing After the Learning

- Did the learner complete the task or tasks successfully?
- What did the student learn?
- What are students' areas of strength and weakness?
- What do the evaluation results show?
- What does the student need next?

Alone

Advantages	Disadvantages
Individual accountability	No opportunity to learn from others
Works at own pace	May practice incorrectly
Works at level of need	Harder to assess each individual
Makes individual choices	No interdependence
Meets intrapersonal needs	More difficult to design specific plans

---

P for Partner

Assessing Before the Teaching

- Which assignments will be most effective in a partner working relationship?
- What is the most advantageous way to form partners?
- Is peer-to-peer tutoring needed?
- How will each partner activity be assessed?
- Is individual accountability built into the plan?

Assessing During the Learning

- Are the partners getting along socially?
- Is each member doing his or her part?
- Are partners staying on task?
- Is the assignment a quality learning experience for each individual?

Assessing After the Partner Experience

- What did each partner learn?
- What does each team need to do next?
- How are partners going to share what they learned?
- Should these students be paired as partners again?

Partner Sharing After the Learning Assessment: Informal

Partner activities engage all learners. When two individuals share, one student talks while the partner listens.

Use ideas similar to the following "noteworthy note spotlights" to make partner assessments productive experiences:

- Individually write a note with two to three things you learned.
- Take your notes, and find a partner.
- Decide who will be Partner A and who will be Partner B.
- Share your notes by taking turns.

Variations
- A partner reads all of his or her notes at one time and then chooses a favorite note to discuss.
- Partners A and B take turns, each sharing one note. Continue until all items are shared.
    1. Partner A shares an item. Partner B then shares one that relates to the item that Partner A shared.

    2. Partner A then shares a note that relates to Partner B's note. They continue taking turns until all notes are shared.

A/B Partners: Sharing-Linking Thinking

This activity allows students to practice linking what they have learned to other facts. Teachers should observe the skill with which students perform this activity. Some instruction, guidance, and practice may be needed to develop this skill.

Each student individually writes two to three things learned. Students meet with their energizing partners and decide who will be Partner A and Partner B. Partner A begins by sharing facts or information. When the teacher claps, Partner B starts with Partner A's last word and continues more thoughts. When the teacher claps again, Partner A begins with the last word from Partner B and links it to other facts related to the topic.

Partners share their written statements as follows:

▲ Partner A shares one item.
▲ Partner B shares one linking item.
▲ Partner A shares a second item that links to Partner B's last thought.
▲ Partner B shares the second linking item.

This continues until the teacher gives a signal. The partners may signal the teacher when they have shared all of the statements related to things they learned. This activity is fun and challenging.

Assessing a Working Partner Team: Comments

1. Are the two students following the directions?   Yes   No
2. Do they have needed materials?   Yes   No
3. Are they working toward their goal?   Yes   No
4. Are they on task?   Yes   No
5. Are they learning information they need?   Yes   No
6. Is the team productive?   Yes   No
7. Are the partners cooperating?   Yes   No
8. The best work of the partner team occurs when _____.

Partner

Advantages	Disadvantages
Provides opportunities for engagement	Shared ownership of a product
Fosters student-focused learning	Difficult to assess individual work
Builds trust	Off-task socializing
Meets interpersonal needs	May not carry equal workload

S for Small Group

Small groups work effectively when all members cooperate to complete the task. Each team member needs specific tasks for individual accountability.

Assessing Before the Teaching

- What are the standards and skills to be learned?
- Which activities will be best for small-group instruction?
- How are the groups to be selected? (e.g., skills, random, alphabetical, interest)
- Will this be a cooperative-learning or a small-group activity?
- How will each group member be held accountable?
- How will each group session be assessed?
- What role will the individuals have?
- Is the small-group arrangement the most effective way to teach the information?
- Are the materials accessible?
- Are the directions clear and precise?

Assessing During the Learning

- Is each group member participating?
- Are group members getting along?
- Is each member doing his or her part?
- Are group members staying on task?
- What else do group members need?
- Are group members learning the content?

Assessing After the Small Group Experience

- Was the group work worth the time?
- What did the group accomplish?
- What will you do differently next time?
- How are group members going to share what they learned?

- Where can the group display the product?
- How will the activity be assessed?

Small Group	
Advantages	**Disadvantages**
Combines views and ideas	Has opportunities to be off task
Focuses on cooperation	Individual accountability is difficult
Teaches tolerance	Unequal sharing of responsibilities
Fosters active student learning	May create power struggles
Meets interpersonal needs	Often dominated by one or two students

EVALUATING GROUP WORK

Table 6.1 is a sample assessment for analyzing the success of a group member. It may be completed by the student, a peer, the group, or the teacher.

Table 6.1   Group Member Assessment Checklist

Name _____   Date _____

Observable Behavior	Not yet	Sometimes	Most of the time	Comments
Stayed on task				
Followed directions				
Showed respect for group members				
Completed his or her share of the work				

Use the scales in Figures 6.4 and 6.5 to evaluate a group. This assessment is designed to be completed by the total group, a group member, or the observing teacher.

Group Discussion: Assessment

Observe the learner during formal and informal group discussion. An effective teacher always strives to draw out the student's best efforts. Many times during group discussions, one student dominates the conversation. Occasionally, it is important to listen without contributing to the discussion. As the accuracy and depth of the information is observed and analyzed, identify who contributes each segment. A learner may not contribute to the discussion because he or she does not have an opportunity to share or because he or she is afraid of being wrong.

Observe the following parts of a discussion scene to assess the quality of the learner's interactions:

- Contributes to the discussion
- Contributions are on task, relevant, and accurate
- Makes a connection between information learned with personal experiences
- Refers to the learned information to support a view, opinion, or comment
- Discusses the information fluently with the group
- Draws conclusions and inferences based on what was learned
- Expresses opinions and ideas freely

Independent Members Score the Group

Provide one form for each group member. As the student scores group work, he or she looks on the original one to see each criterion. After scoring each item, the student writes a comment to validate his or her rationale for giving a particular score.

Self-Assessment for a Group Member

The checklist in Figure 6.5 is designed to help each group member to think about his or her participation, contributions, and teamwork during the assignment. Select items from the checklist that are appropriate to the situation.

(Text continues on p. 160)

Figure 6.4   Evaluating Group Work. The following group work assessment tool can be used by the group, a group member, or the observing teacher.

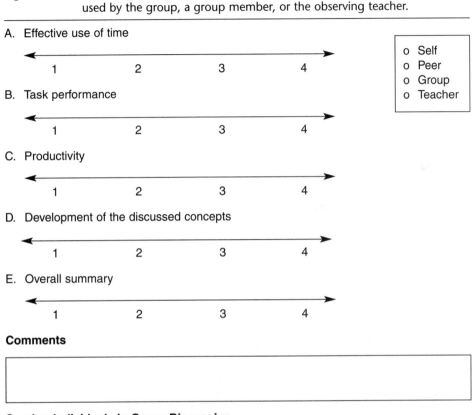

A. Effective use of time

    1   2   3   4

o Self
o Peer
o Group
o Teacher

B. Task performance

    1   2   3   4

C. Productivity

    1   2   3   4

D. Development of the discussed concepts

    1   2   3   4

E. Overall summary

    1   2   3   4

Comments

Scoring Individuals in Group Discussion

Use the previous summary scale to complete a roster of individual scores as an assessment tool.

Name					Strengths and Needs
_____	1	2	3	4	_____
_____	1	2	3	4	_____
_____	1	2	3	4	_____

Comments

Observer's Signature _____   Date _____

Figure 6.5 Self-Assessment for a Group Participant

Name of Activity _____   Date _____

Student _____   Rater _____

	Yes	Sometimes	No

1. I was needed in my group.

2. I helped others if I could, and they needed me.

3. I listened to the discussion.

4. I respected other members of my group.

5. I shared my ideas.

6. I felt that my ideas were accepted.

7. I encouraged other members of my group.

8. I was treated with respect by group members.

   A. The best thing about our group is _____.

   B. We need to improve on _____.

   C. Other suggestions and comments

Signature _____ Date _____

Figure 6.6   Assessment of Group Work by an Individual Student

Individual group members use the following form to assess other members of the group. Remind everyone to make comments that are suggestions for improvement.
Name of scoring group member _____

Name		Low				High
_____ A.	1	2	3	4	Why? _____
_____ B.	1	2	3	4	Why? _____
_____ C.	1	2	3	4	Why? _____
_____ D.	1	2	3	4	Why? _____

Overall Group Summary   1   2   3   4

Why? _____

Comments:

Signature _____   Date _____

Group Design

Use various flexible grouping designs in diverse ways to find the best way to organize students for assessment tasks. Assess the situation and the tasks frequently to plan the best opportunity for the learner. Change groups as needed.

Use the following questions as guidelines to make flexible grouping decisions:

- The grouping design that works best for this task is _____.
- Do I need to use the same design for all, or should I use different designs to meet an individual student's needs?
- What are the most effective working teams for this assignment?
- Who is working with whom?
- Where is the best place for each group to work?
- How will the roles be assigned to the different groups?

- What rules, directions, and guidelines need to be established?
- What materials will each group need to complete the task?
- What worked well the last time I grouped these students into working teams?

Choose the grouping design based on the standard and the purpose. Assign the students based on their individual needs. Analyze the task and the amount of time needed to complete it. Group the members by their ability to get the job done.

Select from a variety of grouping designs when planning assessment activities. Use multiage, knowledge, interest, random, or ability groups to work on specific new skills, to review information, or to learn new concepts. Consider the following choices.

Knowledge-Based Groups

Knowledge-based groups are formed according to each student's background and previous experience with the topic or skill, determined by one or more preassessment tools. The results identify the student's readiness or entry level for a particular study. During the preassessment analysis, the student's trouble spots are identified and then addressed in instructional plans. The grouping design is selected to meet the challenge of the task and to expand each member's knowledge base. The individual student's learning potential increases because he or she is challenged on the appropriate level for success.

Interests Groups

The teacher can provide opportunities for students to form groups by signing up for their areas of interest in a unit of study, or the results of interest inventories and surveys can be used to make group assignments. When a student demonstrates an interest in a subject, he or she will usually "buy in," or have a strong desire to study and work with others with related materials and resources.

Ability Groups

Ability grouping is a traditional grouping design that has been used for many years. Evidence of a student's ability is gathered from preassessments. The individual is grouped with other learners on the same ability level.

At one time teachers formed ability groups at the beginning of the year, and those students stayed together in the group for the entire school year. Some ability groups were named after birds: Bluebirds and Redbirds were common group names. Once a group was formed, a student was trapped at that level, so "once a buzzard, always a buzzard" became common practice. Today this is not true. Ability groups are formed as needed to teach specific skills and concepts. The student moves on to a more challenging group after information and skills are mastered.

Random Groups

If a task can be easily completed by all class members, random grouping is the way to go. Choose one of the following sample ideas for novel, random grouping designs:

- Count off students using the numbers 1 through 7 to form seven groups. The 1s work together; the 2s work together; and so on.
- Select names from a hat to form each group.
- Mix Match: Choose four or five topics. Write three or four pieces of information about each topic on separate cards. Ask students to find the people in the room who have information about the same topic to form groups.
- Choose four animals. Write four attributes for each animal on separate cards. Ask students to find the other cardholders who complete the set.
- Make cards using objects, numerals, shapes, or colors, and place the words to match them on separate cards. Ask each individual to draw a card and team up with students with a matching card.
- Draw strings. Choose five colors of yarn, and cut each into equal pieces. Place the strings in a bag. Ask students to draw strings and form groups with the matching colors.

Peer-to-Peer Tutoring

This grouping design works best if peers respect each other and get along socially. Often a peer team is formed because one student has a stronger knowledge base or ability. The other student needs to learn or work more with the information. One learner teaches or tutors the other student. Be careful not to overuse a particular student as a tutor. The student who knows the information needs time to learn more about the topic. Tutoring sessions must be beneficial for both students. The best peer tutor is the student who has had a "lightbulb comment." This individual is excited when called upon to share or teach this information to someone else. Teaching information is one of the best ways to crystallize the learning in the mind. If I teach it, I learn it!

Cooperative Groups

Cooperative teams are formed to complete a common task. Each team member has a role with at least one responsibility to carry out during the group work. The members have shared power and are individually accountable for the assigned responsibility. The group or team uses consensus to make decisions. Teams need to practice working together several times to create bonds, develop respect, and build team spirit. Teachers should discuss with students the social outcomes as well as the cognitive development and learning expected from cooperative teams.

Multiage Groups

In multiage groups, an older student is paired with a younger student. This design works well if the students have an opportunity to create bonds and develop mutual respect for each other. Often students have to be explicitly taught how to work together. Model and discuss cooperation in detail. Practice in mock simulations. Over time the students usually develop a good working relationship in which both students share responsibility in discussions and tasks.

Multiage groups are effective because the younger student often looks up to the older student as an academic and social role model. The older student develops confidence and a sense of responsibility and pride.

A multiage group may be composed of students of different ages to participate in an activity, a discussion, a task, or a project. Group members may be selected by common interests, by academic needs, or by random selection. These groups work in multiage classrooms, with buddy classes, or across grade levels.

Troubleshooting Tools for Group Assessment

If negative or inappropriate behavior occurs during a group assessment, it must be corrected quickly and quietly to avoid interrupting the work of other students. The following ideas are designed as troubleshooting tools to use during group assessment activities.

What to do when a student . . .

Acts Negatively Most of the Time

- Brainstorm positive words and phrases.
- Model positive ways to make comments and responses.
- Smile and show your approval when positive behavior is observed.
- Engage the student in pleasant friendly conversation about the problem, and come to solutions.
- Volunteer to be a sounding board for the student's complaints so the two of you can solve the problems together.

Says or Does Something With Which You Do Not Agree

- Listen to the student's opinion, and remain open.
- Express your point of view in a friendly, neutral way, if appropriate.
- Remember that "your way or the highway" will not lead to mutual understanding.

Has a Personality Clash With a Group Member

- Consider separating students, if the behavior is long term.
- Schedule a conference, and provide tips for the students to work it out together.
- Acknowledge the student's preference to work alone, but coach the student in how to work with others when it is necessary.
- Design assignments that give each group member at least one responsibility.
- Take time to discuss the value of positive, appropriate behaviors at the end of activities.

Often Has to Be "Spoon-Fed" Information

- Identify how the student learns best, and use his or her strengths to build confidence.
- Give directions in smaller increments or "chunks."
- Use specific praise for growth and improvement.

Adding new models or an exciting strategy is both exciting and challenging for teacher and students as they move toward differentiated learning and assessment. Before introducing a new idea, read and reread the related material. Choose the assessment tools to use. Identify possible challenge areas, and decide how to address each one. Then step out bravely into the new teaching and learning format.

Differentiating Assessment in the Age of Accountability

7

Our current reliance on test scores as the measure of both one's intelligence and one's academic success assumes both that human beings can be labeled and categorized based on a series of decontextualized, paper-and-pencil exercises and that learning can be reduced to a mechanical process with clear-cut goals and definable outcomes, much like the process of producing a car on an assembly line in Detroit.

(Lazear, 1999, p. xiv)

Essential Question: How can the diverse needs of learners be accommodated during formal assessments?

◆

STANDARDIZED ASSESSMENT

Teachers are required to comply with local, state, and national standards related to assessment and are held accountable for their students' scores on standardized tests. These requirements must be aligned with the mandated goals and expectations. School districts must demonstrate the academic success of students on their annual reports of Adequate Yearly Progress.

The No Child Left Behind Act (NCLB) mandates that school districts meet assessment requirements, reporting procedures, and accountability standards. The federal government monitors the schools' progress and compliance through the National Assessment of Educational Progress. Schools that fail to make the grade must submit a plan for improvement. If progress is not reflected within two years, the schools may become charter or magnet schools. Students in one of these failing schools may move to another school or request funded special services (Bloomfield & Cooper, 2003). If the school continues to have a failing program, federal support decreases. These funding sanctions affect the school's basic functioning and staffing.

NCLB legislation has brought more attention to student assessment. Teachers and school administrators are more accountable for test results. The standards, benchmarks, and objectives have become the focus of teaching and learning.

The U.S. education secretary has detailed components of what works to increase student achievement and create success. Educational practice and materials must align with the following criteria:

- The use of scientifically proven methods
- Aligned standards
- Assessment and instruction
- School and district focus on student learning
- Accountability for results
- Highly qualified teachers

How does differentiated assessment meet accountability standards? Educators use this approach to identify the individual students' needs and strengths to plan appropriate instruction. Differentiated instruction and assessment address educational standards with novel, intriguing strategies and skills in the diverse ways students learn.

The goal of differentiated assessment is to provide each student with tools he or she can easily and automatically recall and apply in academic tasks and daily activities. As students are presented with assessment activities, they are provided with opportunities to become reflective, self-assessing, internally directed learners, capable of reaching their fullest learning potentials.

Differentiated assessment also provides teachers with an ongoing loop of assessment data to inform decisions regarding instruction and learning. Differentiation assists individual students in succeeding with standards and in making yearly progress.

The Impact of High-Stakes Testing

The term *high-stakes testing* refers to the major impact the results have on students, teachers, schools, communities, counties, states, or the nation. Here are a few examples of the many ways test scores impact stakeholders.

Students

- Test results are used to make pass-fail decisions.
- Graduation depends on test success.
- Participation in sports is denied to individuals with low grades.
- Acceptance or rejection in special classes depends on the scores.
- Students with low scores often become discouraged and drop out of school.

Teachers

- In some states, salary incentives and sanctions are based on improved scores.
- Colleagues feel pressured as scores are publicized and compared.
- Less time is available to create activities for students to experience the joy of learning.
- Mandated improvement programs for higher test results bring stress and anxiety to teachers who have low-performing students.
- The test objectives are aligned with state standards and skills.

Schools

- Test scores of schools in the district and state are compared.
- Sanctions on low-achieving schools result in less federal funding.
- Improvement programs are mandated to improve test scores.

Community

- Parents avoid purchasing homes in areas with low-performing schools.
- Families move out of neighborhoods with low-performing schools.
- Students are moved to private schools, resulting in less pubic school funding.
- Businesses move into areas with high-performing test takers.

HOW CAN STANDARDIZED ASSESSMENTS BE DIFFERENTIATED?

Standardized assessments contain specific guidelines and directions in the teacher's guide or manual. These formal assessments contain specific requirements. The district or school administrator may establish additional guidelines or procedures.

The guidelines set forth in standardized assessment and directives from the district and school-site administrators must be followed.

Fortunately, there are several aspects of standardized assessments that have no restrictions. This autonomy gives the teacher opportunities to differentiate assessment. As preparations are made to implement the mandated regulations, the teacher needs to look for ways to differentiate in areas that enhance the individual student's opportunities to succeed.

Each student approaches tests with different attitudes, skills, and expectations for success. Standardized assessments, however, are administered with the same directions, time limits, response formats, and questions. There is little reference to the diverse student learning styles in the classroom.

Encourage students to share their personal needs for top assessment performances. Read the requirements and guidelines for each test before accommodating the students' needs through differentiated assessment.

Accommodations: In the Teacher's Hands

It is not possible to accommodate all learners during standardized tests because of formal procedures and guidelines. These rules and regulations are out of the teacher's hands, or realm of control. Thoroughly review the directions that accompany an assessment before considering student accommodations. Identify the specific factors that are *out* of the teacher's hands. List the factors related to the assessment experience that are *in* the teacher's control. These factors may be adjusted to accommodate individual needs.

Use the following suggestions and tips to differentiate for individual students during assessment experiences. Implement changes during routine testing sessions, so the students become comfortable with them. For example, move the desks apart, and make accommodations during chapter and unit tests.

Seating

- Provide opportunities for students to choose comfortable places to work.
- Make a specific seating assignment to meet an individual's need.
- Space the desks to allow free movement for monitoring.

Time

- If possible, decide how many tests to administer each day, and select the most appropriate time to give them.
- Plan brief periods of enjoyable, physical activity in fresh air to rejuvenate the students' brains. If it is not possible to go outside between assessment segments, engage the students in challenging but relaxing activities in high-interest areas.

- If possible, administer assessment when the students are most alert. For example, research reveals that high school students are most alert in the afternoon.

Tools

- Provide the tools the student needs to be successful if they fit within the assessment rules and guidelines. For example, a student's comprehension may improve if he or she is allowed to use a reading guide, such as an index card, ruler, or marker as he or she reads the directions.
- Make scratch paper, calculators, pencils, placeholders, pencil grips, and erasers available.
- Refer to #2 test-taking pencils throughout the year as "smart pencils." Use smart pencils and other novel tools to entice the student during assessment sessions.

Personal Needs

- Provide a privacy cubicle to a student who is easily distracted.
- Separate students who are peer-dependent.
- Identify students who have special needs that require specific equipment and have it available for the assessment.

Create a Positive Testing Environment

Teachers, administrators, and parents prepare and encourage students to do their best on tests. At the same time they may unintentionally create barriers to the students' success by creating test-taking fears and anxieties. The emphasis on test results places more pressure on everyone associated with the school. In turn, the drive for higher test scores places more pressure on students.

Brain research and common sense tells us that the brain functions best when in a relaxed, nonthreatened state. The brain cannot devote its total thinking capacity to benefit the student when it is coping with fear of failure, anxiety, and stress.

A positive testing environment establishes a learning climate for optimal brain functioning. Think about the phrase *positive testing environment*. Does this sound like an oxymoron to you? Are the words *positive* and *testing* incompatible terms? Teachers and administrators need to be aware of negative comments, activities, and actions in the school and home that create barriers to test success. They must develop specific plans to create a positive testing environment that leads each student to view assessments as valuable experiences that will expedite the learning journey.

> We believe everyone should view tests as celebrations of the brain's phenomenal abilities, not as dreaded events. (Chapman & King, 2000, p. xi)

GIVE EFFECTIVE DIRECTIONS

It is not uncommon for a teacher to complete assessment instructions and immediately see a student with his or her hand raised to ask the frustrating question, "Now what am I supposed to do?" Why does this happen?

Use the following tip to keep this from occurring. Give directions immediately before students are to carry them out. Also, remember to make the directions as short and clear as possible. It may be necessary to give one or two steps at a time for a procedure. This improves comprehension, clarifies the message, and paces tasks. Ask various students to repeat the directions as they heard them so the teacher can modify or clarify for understanding.

Standardized test directions usually require the teacher to read test directions exactly as printed. If so, read in a clear, distinct, friendly voice with verbal emphasis on important directional information. If possible, review the directions in advance, and practice reading them.

Direction Variations

When giving assessments, it is important that directions are clearly understood. They should be purposeful and fully explained, so students can carry them out with ease and correctness. Throughout the year, vary assessment directions to provide students with practice in working with the same information in different ways. When directions are varied, students who have difficulty with one approach have opportunities to respond to the information in another way. See the show-and-tell variations in Chapter 4.

TEACH TEST-TAKING SKILLS

Teachers must analyze the demands of tests and determine how to embed the test-taking skills in classroom activities. They must know how to assist students during the year as they learn the specific skills needed with various test formats.

Self-Regulated Skills Needed for Test Success

Teach students to use self-regulation skills during tests. Remind them to keep their mental wheels turning and on the right track!

- Listen for key words.
- Control your thinking.
- Concentrate on the tasks you need to complete.
- Monitor your time, so you can pace the work.

Stumped and Stalled

Show learners how to use strategies similar to the following when they have difficulty with a test item or when they don't know the answer to a question:

- Look for clues.
- Visualize yourself as you were learning this information.
- Reword or simplify the directions.
- Chunk it! Place the information in a category or group.
- Compare or contrast it with a familiar object or person.
- Read the directions without the unknown word.
- Replace the unknown word with a familiar word.

Breakthrough Clues for Reading Directions

Teach students to look for Breakthrough Clues in the test directions if they have difficulty understanding what to do.

Be a Spy for Words That Qualify

A qualifying word intensifies, modifies, or limits the meaning of another word or phrase. Emphasize the importance of being a spy for words that qualify, because they can change the meaning of a statement or question.

always	all	never	none	only	true	false
except	more than	less than	some	negative	many	positive

Note the Negatives

Prefixes change or modify the meaning of words. Teach students to be aware of the prefixes that create a negative word or phrase in the test directions.

un	non	in	ill	dis	im

Thinking Term Gab

Throughout the year, make assessment terms easy for students to understand and use. Provide opportunities for students to apply the terms as they work with the information and show what they know. Use the terms simultaneously when creating assignments and in isolation so students associate the terms with the simpler meanings. In Table 7.1 the word or phrase beside each term is designed to assist students with an understanding of the task's

Table 7.1   Thinking Terms

Evaluation	Synthesis	Analysis
• Judge: take a guess • Confirm: show how it is true • Predict: make a guess • Evaluate: give the value • Choose	• Design: develop • Compose: create an original • Construct: build • Illustrate: draw • Propose: suggest • Organize: put in order • Plan: map out • Classify: place in groups • Invent: use your ideas	• Compare: name ways they are the same • Contrast: name ways they are different • Question: ask about it • Debate: give your side of an argument • Solve: find the answer • Investigate: explore details • Analyze: take it apart and explain • Classify: put in a category • Tell facts and evidence
Application	**Comprehension**	**Knowledge**
• Demonstrate: show how • Apply: use • Assemble: put together • Operate: run it or make it work • Schedule: place in a time slot • Practice: do it again to make it easier for you • Translate: put it in easier words	• Discuss: talk about it • Brainstorm thoughts and opinions • Describe: give details that tell about it • Picture in a few sentences • Report • Summarize: tell the important parts or overall meaning	• List: write it down • Record: place in writing • Define: give the meaning • Locate: find • Review: go over it again • Choose: select • Sequence: place in order

SOURCE: Adapted from Chapman and King (2003b, pp. 44, 45).

purpose. Familiarize students with all of these thinking processes, not only to prepare them for terms they may find in formal assessments, but to strengthen their skills as reflective learners and thinkers.

Check, Check, Check

Rehearse the following self-talk questions until students automatically use them during tests.

- Is my work legible?
- Did I copy the information correctly on the answer sheet?
- Does my answer make sense?
- Are my answer spaces correctly marked or filled in?

GRADING

Whole books can be and have been written about grading. It is a controversial and emotional topic in many ways. This small section offers just a few guidelines to consider in the classroom that differentiates learning and assessment. Give students a combination of informal and formal grades. Use the results from the assignments that reveal the student's knowledge base and some assignments based on his or her ability level. Grades recorded on report cards represent the student's academic ability as reflected in his or her performance and ability related to the subject.

Behavior, effort, and attitude are not indicators of ability and performance. Of course, these factors influence learning and may accompany the academic report, but they need to appear in a separate section or form.

There will always be subjectivity in grades. Gather as much solid evidence as possible, and give the grade that reflects the evidence. If the grade is borderline, the teacher must do what is best for the student.

The Final Grade

Obtain some grades from the student's work when he or she is performing at his or her knowledge base level. For students with readiness below grade level, these grades will be high, because the student understands and is ready for this information. Add grades from his or her work on independent assignments that are on the same level as other class members. For many students, this will bring the grade down because they do not perform as well on grade-level work. Provide some grades based on the student's readiness level and some grades on his or her grade level to provide an overall, unbiased picture of the learner.

> In the differentiated classroom, there must be a combination of assessments so that a true picture of the student's performance is given in the final grade. (Chapman & King, 2003a, p. 191)

These grades reflect the student's current level of work as well as the expectation level. This grading process is fair, too, because it reveals a true picture of the student's performance in relation to the standards at that grade level.

Parent Conferencing to Report Assessment

Plan a parent conference to gain their support as partners in the student's education program. Remember, many parents are intimidated by teachers. Create a cordial atmosphere. Let the parents know that they are major contributors to their student's success.

Use the following sandwich technique to introduce weak areas. Begin the session with praise for the student, and then approach the area of need with a clear, specific description and work samples. Make specific suggestions of ways the student can improve. Close the session with genuine praise for the student. This approach sandwiches negative comments between two or more positive statements. Give the parents specific suggestions to assist, encourage, and support the learner.

Use the following guidelines to organize conference procedures.

1. Carefully review the data you have gathered, especially your student's portfolio and the teacher's observation notes.

2. Begin the conference with a focus on two to three of the student's academic and personal strengths.

3. Avoid reviewing past negative behaviors unless they continue to influence current performance.

4. Identify and discuss the learner's areas of need.

5. Provide specific examples of activities to practice at home.

6. End the conference with positive comments.

7. Remind parents to use the student's strengths to strengthen his or her weaker areas.

   Examples:

   A. If the student enjoys artwork, encourage him or her to create illustrations for skills or concepts.
   B. If the student enjoys movement activities, encourage him or her to act out the skill or concept.

8. Emphasize the emotional barriers created by negative comments and actions.

9. Encourage parents to use positive comments that support and motivate the learner.

10. Praise the parents for taking their valuable time to participate in the conference.

In this age of accountability, we must always remember that the goal of assessment is to identify ways to assist individual learners. Students should know that each assessment tool is designed to gather information for their improvement.

Pulling It All Together: Planning Differentiated Assessment

8

> *The object of education is to prepare the young to educate themselves throughout their lives.*
>
> —Robert Maynard Hutchins

Essential Question: What are the most effective ways to organize and plan incorporation of differentiated assessment strategies?

As has been emphasized throughout this resource, assessment is an evolving, ongoing process that occurs throughout the teaching process. This chapter investigates and tackles strategic planning for differentiated assessment. This is essential in meeting the diverse needs of learners. Teachers must be consciously aware of the assessment strategies and tools embedded in instruction. The following step-by-step chart, Figure 8.1, and the accompanying discussion of planning are intended to serve as a guide to the ongoing assessment procedures that drive instruction.

◆

IMPLEMENTATION PLAN FOR ASSESSMENT

Use the following detailed step-by-step procedure as a guide to ongoing assessment procedures that drive instruction. Figure 8.1 contains a condensed version of this procedure to further explain the plan.

Figure 8.1   An Implementation Plan for Quality-Differentiated Assessment

9. Assess After the Learning
Identify the information and skills the student learned. Ask, "What does the student need next?" Use this information to set new instructional goals.

8. Strategically Readjust the Plan
This is the time to revisit, revamp, and adjust the plan to meet individualsí needs.

7. Teach the Plan
Continue to monitor and assess student learning related to the plan during instruction. Continue to use ongoing assessment to gather and use information.

6. Assess the Plan
Label the targeted intelligences to determine if they address the learners' modalities, diverse skills, and abilities. Analyze the flexible grouping designs to be sure they create an accurate flow of activities and strategies.

5. Design a Quality Plan
Choose the best strategies and activities from the brainstormed list for this particular student or group. Design a quality plan for instruction that meets the identified needs and interests.

4. Brainstorm a Quantity of Activities
List all possible activities and strategies to teach this information to the individual or group of students to meet the specific needs identified in the data analysis.

3. Compile and Analyze the Preassessment Data
Examine and interpret the data. Use the gathered information to identify the learnersí entry points for instruction

2. Select the Tool and Preassess the Student
Find out what the learner knows: his or her background, prior knowledge, interests, and experiences related to the selected skill or information.

1. Determine What to Teach
Identify the specific standard, skill, indicator, or benchmark to teach. Set goals.

Adapt the following Implementation Plan for Assessment to meet the needs of your students:

1. Determine What to Teach. Choose the unit of focus.

   Select what you are going to teach.

   Identify the standard, concept, topic, benchmark, or skill to be assessed.

2. Select the assessment tool and preassess the student.

   Determine how to preassess the learner's knowledge base.

   What tool or tools will be used?

   Is the tool an informal or formal assessment?

   Does the assessment need to address the affective domain, the cognitive domain, or both?

   Identify the student's knowledge base, interests, and attitudes.

   What does the student know at the beginning of the learning?

   What are the student's attitudes and feelings related to the learning?

3. Compile and analyze the assessment data.

   Compile the data from the preassessment to gather information about the learner's past experiences and background. If the learner's prior knowledge and experiences are positive, the student usually has a yearning to learn more. In a positive state, the student's mind resembles a sponge, ready to absorb the information. New learning builds on the emotions and feelings developed from past experiences with related opportunities. If the student sees a need to learn, perceives the information or skill as meaningful, relevant, and interesting, learning occurs. If the learner has had bad experiences or difficulties with previous information in the area of study, the learning is more difficult. It is important for the teacher to be aware of the past experiences to build on the foundation of knowledge as well as attitudes and desires of the individual student.

   Determine the skills or information the student needs to learn next. Examine the student's knowledge level and what he or she needs to learn next. Fill in the learning gaps that may be barriers to understanding. Too often this important step in planning is omitted. Start the student at his or her knowledge base and move along the learning continuum, according to the student's individual needs. Fill in the gaps. If no holes exist, enhace the student's knowledge, skills, or interests. Use these essential keys to identify the starting place, or entry points, for learning.

Educators have been heard to remark, "You are in the _____ grade. You should know this," or, "You were suppose to learn this in _____ grade." When it is obvious that a student missed important information, the teacher must move the student from where he or she is and build the foundation for learning by adding to his or her skills and knowledge base. It is up to both the teacher and the student to make this happen. The best time for any student to gain knowledge or skills he or she missed is now. Remember, it is never too late to learn.

4. Brainstorm a quantity or variety of activities to teach.

Prepare a list of all the instructional strategies and activities that can be used to teach the information. This is a list of significant quantity that gives the teacher a large amount of options from which to choose. This process is very effective when teams of teacher brainstorm the list. Each teacher then selects the effective approaches, the most engaging and interesting activities from the list for his particular group of students. These strategically chosen activities and strategies are effective, quality ways to teach the information to his unique group of students.

5. Design a quality plan by placing the strategies and activities in sequence to create a quality lesson plan. Lay out the plan to analyze the quality of the assessment's quality. Determine the most effective and efficient order for teaching the activities, concepts, and strategies. Examine the lesson plan sequence for flow, relevance, and need.

6. Assesses the plan. Provide for differentiation by planning a variety of strategies and activities that give students opportunities to work with the information in their own way.

   a. Label the styles and intelligences of the activities or strategies in your lesson plan.
      Examples: V/L=Verbal/Linguistic M/R=Musical/Rhythmic
      (See Multiple Intelligences in Chapter 3.)

b. Fix the "Big O's," the overkills and omissions. When the labeling is complete, decide if there are too many activities under one intelligence target. For example, if a math unit, standard, concept, or benchmark being planned, check to see if most of the activities target the Logical/Mathematical intelligence? If so, refer to the original brainstormed list to find activities or strategies that target other intelligences. If a way of learning is omitted, think of an effective activity that will teach the information or refer to the original list of activities and strategies.

c. Select the appropriate flexible grouping designs.

T = Total Group   A = Alone   P = Partner   S = Small Group

Label activities in the plan by using the previous symbols to determine an appropriate blend of grouping scenarios. By doing this, you assess whether the students are working alone or with others through the study sequence. For example, if the students work on the activity in a small group and then work with the information alone, label this activity "SA" for small group and alone.

7. Teach the plan. Continue to gather assessment data during the lesson. Be aware of individual and group needs. Whenever possible, provide immediate feedback and guidance to avoid gaps in learning.

a. Decide if you need to revamp, review, reteach, move on, enrich, enhance.

b. Identify boring parts, frustrating points, or challenging opportunities that appear during the learning.

c. Decide how and when to use student self-reflection activities.

d. Incorporate celebration events into the learning plan.

8. Strategically readjust the plan by revamping, enhancing, and revisiting skills or information to meet individual needs.

9. Assess after the learning by identifying what an individual or group needs to learn. Ask yourself questions similar to the following to guide new instructional plans:

a. Did the student master the skills, standards, or objectives?

b. What does the student need to learn next?

c. What can be carried over to the next unit?

d. What will I teach next?

CONTENT, PROCESS, PRODUCT, AND LEARNING DISPOSITIONS ASSESSMENT

According to Carol Ann Tomlinson (1999), there are at least three components that work hand in hand in a differentiated classroom: content, process, and product. She identifies these as commonalities to differentiate for learning, and therefore assess. We also include the student's learning dispositions, a category which includes attitude, habits of mind and work, abilities—all of the elements that make up the holistic learner. We have added disposition as a major area for assessment because of its profound influence on the results. We place assessment as the centerpiece. Teachers assess the content, how the student processes the information and how the product shows evidence of what the student has learned. The teacher can use the chart in Figure 8.2 to plan the assessments for these elements.

Process Assessment Tools

Process assessment tools reveal how evidence or data is gathered over time. The assessment tool may analyze the learner's level of engagement in specific learning. The student tells or demonstrates his or her step-by-step thinking processes. This shows how the student is mentally manipulating information. When the learner processes orally, it is easier to identify mistakes for correction and success for celebration. This procedure reveals the learner's unique and personal way of approaching problems and situations.

Process assessment tools answer the following question during the planning phase of instruction: How will the students learn this information?

Examples

- Tell how you got the answer.
- Show each step. Explain what you did on each one and why.

Product Assessment Tools

Product assessment tools are administered at one time and create a result that can be examined. For example, when a rubric is presented as a guideline at the beginning of a project assignment, the student and teacher know and understand the expectations and requirements of the assignment. The score is based on the product or evidence gathered.

Examples

- Create a rap, rhyme, or jingle that describes the new geometric shapes.
- Design a travel brochure for your favorite vacation destination.

Figure 8.2 Content, Process, Product, and Behavior Assessment

Tool	Content	Process	Product	Learning Dispositions	Date	Date	Date
Anecdotal Records							
Center Activities							
Computerized Programs							
Conferences							
Conversations							
Demonstrations							
Inventories							
Journal Entries							
Likert Scales							
Literary Circles							
Logs							
Metacognitive Questions							
Observations							
Portfolios							
Presentations							
Projects							
Reports							
Rubrics							
Standardized Tests							
Surveys							
Teacher-Made Tests							
Text Talks							
Topic-Related Activities							

Content Assessment Tools

Content assessment tools gather evidence of the knowledge, progress, understanding, and growth that occur during the teaching of a unit, topic, or standard. For example, a unit portfolio is a content assessment tool because it consists of work samples gathered throughout a topic of study. It provides evidence of the child's growth and needs related to his or her understanding of the standard, content, skill, or information.

Examples

- What have you learned about the country you studied?
- Read a book, article, or brochure related to the country. Which facts do you need to remember?

Learning Disposition Assessment Tools

Learning disposition assessment tools gather evidence about the student's attitudes, feelings, behavior, and interests. For example, an individual checklist in a cooperative learning activity records a team member's social interactions and level of participation.

The Full Planning Toolbox

Use Figure 8.3 to select the appropriate tools for planning differentiated assessment. For each tool you plan to use, enter the approximate date you plan to use it, and note the following code in the planning box for your assessment purpose:

F = Formal assessment

I = Informal assessment

In some instances you may be using the same tool for multiple purposes. Use and adapt the key code above to keep track of your plan. You may choose to use the same tool at different times for different purposes. Use the code again, and put dates or checks in the boxes to record your plan.

BEFORE THE LEARNING: PREASSESSMENT

Preassessment is an essential prerequisite for effective diagnosis and planning. The teacher preassesses the learner's knowledge base and experiences in relation to the upcoming standard, topic, or skill. The information gathered establishes the starting point for planning the learning experiences. Teachers who strategically administer preassessments before planning lessons ensure that the student's strengths and needs are addressed.

(Text continues on page 196)

Figure 8.3   Assessment Tools and Strategies at Work: Planning Differentiated Assessment

Tools and Strategies	Chapter	Before	During	After	Planning Notes
Make Personal Connections	1				
Foster Intelligent Behaviors	1				
Yuk Spots	2				
Bright Spots	2				
Yuk Spots/Bright Spots Scavenger Hunt	2				
Teacher Assessment of the Classroom Environment	2				
Climate Goals: An Implementation Grid	2				
Emotional Intelligences With Indicators	2				
Assessment Guides Planning	3				
Meet the Intelligences	3				
Tear Into Your Intelligences	3				
Pause and Ponder!	3				
Analyzing Interest	3				
Student Reflection Samples	3				
Intelligences and You	3				
Getting to Know *Me:* An Object View	3				
Conceal and Reveal	3				
Other Ways to View Learners	3				

Tools and Strategies	Chapter	Before	During	After	Planning Notes
Statements to Open and Close the Mind	3				
True Colors	3				
Engagement/ Disengagement Spectrum	3				
Unacceptable Behaviors/ Valued Behaviors	3				
Tips to Promote Positive Feelings for Assessments	3				
Dependent and Independent Behaviors	3				
Four Ways of Knowing	3				
Conceal and Reveal	3				
I'm All That Hat	3				
Put Up and Pass	3				
My Silhouette Featurette	3				
Shadow Show	3				
Show Your True Colors	3				
An Objective View of Learners	3				
Four Ways of Knowing and Showing	3				
Observation Criteria	3				
Learning Performance Levels	3				
Preassessment Previews	3				
Ponder and Pass	3				
Duo Response Cards	3				
Triple Response Cards	3				
Prompts to Learn About Students From Other Cultures	3				

Tools and Strategies	Chapter	Before	During	After	Planning Notes
Sample Survey Questions	3				
Assessing Oral Comprehension	3				
Learning Performance Levels	3				
Preassessment Previews	4				
Ponder and Pass	4				
Duo Response Cards	4				
Triple Response Cards	4				
Four-Way Responses	4				
Content Response Cards	4				
Show-and-Tell	4				
Take a Stand	4				
Gold Goal Band	4				
Knowledge Base Corners	4				
Attitude Corners	4				
Interest Corners	4				
Mystery Masters	4				
Content Knowledge Boxes	4				
Developing Questions for Surveys	4				
Brainstorming Guidelines	4				
Color Clusters	4				
Take a Number	4				
Gallimaufry Gatherings	4				

Tools and Strategies	Chapter	Before	During	After	Planning Notes
Develop the Pretest	4				
Baggie Tools	4				
Game Pieces	4				
Cash In	4				
Puzzling Problems	4				
Word Scavenge	4				
Sticky Tab Tag	4				
Dots, Stickers, Stars	4				
Double Duty	4				
Musical Notes	4				
Color Coding	4				
Taking Notes	4				
Tab With Color	4				
Color Overlays	4				
Design Delights	4				
Shape It	4				
Drawings	4				
Self-Talk	4				
The Brain's Speech Bubble	4				
Gallimaufry Gathering Grid	4				
Open-Ended Questions	5				
Self-Reflective Prompts	5				
Rubric for Scoring Open-Ended Questions	5				
Questions to Use After Learning	5				

Tools and Strategies	Chapter	Before	During	After	Planning Notes
Lead-ins to Analysis and Reflection	5				
Key Words From Bloom's Taxonomy for Questioning on Various Thinking Levels	5				
Tally Table	5				
Observation Chart	5				
Bus Stop	5				
Evening Learning Opportunities (ELOs)	5				
Workable Likert Scales	5				
Progress Likert Scales	5				
Rubric Hodgepodge	5				
Rubric Form Samples	5				
Oral Report Rubric Form	5				
Progress Rubric	5				
Rubric to Score Open-Ended Questions	5				
Weighted Rubrics	5				
Rubric for Independent Work	5				
Checklists for Observing and Monitoring	5				
Developing a Checklist	5				
Checklist for the Checklist	5				
Checklist for Independent Work	5				
Checklist for Observation	5				
Checklist for the Teacher	5				
Oral Reading Assessment	5				

Tools and Strategies	Chapter	Before	During	After	Planning Notes
Check Comprehension	5				
Writing Sample Scoring	5				
Prompts for Writing	5				
Assessing a Written Assessment	5				
Individual Observation Checklist	5				
Assessment for Manipulatives	5				
Recording Anecdotal Notes	5				
Tips for Using Anecdotal Notes	5				
Teacher-Made Tests	5				
Checklist to Analyze the Value of the Checklist	5				
Formats for Teacher-Made Tests	5				
True/False Tests	5				
Multiple Choice	5				
Short Answer	5				
Extended Answers	5				
Performance Tests	5				
Skills Test	5				
Investigative Assessment	5				
Assessing With a Blank Page	5				
Portfolios: What to Use	5				
Designing the Portfolio	5				
Portfolio Briefs	5				

Tools and Strategies	Chapter	Before	During	After	Planning Notes
Designing Portfolio Brief Centers	5				
Showcase Scoring for Portfolios	5				
Rearview Thinking	5				
Using Agendas	6				
Agenda Sample Forms	6				
Assessing the Agenda Plan	6				
Cubing	6				
Designing a Cubing Activity	6				
Choice Boards	6				
Choice Boards for Various Levels and Stages	6				
Flexible Designs for Choice Boards	6				
Assessment Choice Board Samples	6				
Curriculum Compacting Model	6				
Using the Compacting Model With the Novice and the Expert	6				
Compacting for Individuals	6				
Compacting for a Grade Level	6				
Group Assessment Checklist	6				
Group Assessment Scale	6				
Assessment of Group Work by an Individual Student	6				

Tools and Strategies	Chapter	Before	During	After	Planning Notes
Contracts	6				
Contract Checklist	6				
Assessing the Contract With a Checklist	6				
Project-Based Model	6				
Assessing the Project Model	6				
Preassessing a Project With a Checklist	6				
Assessing a Postproject Display	6				
Problem-Based Model Design	6				
Centers, Labs, Stations	6				
Establishing an Exploratory Center	6				
Establishing a Structured Center	6				
Center Management Tips	6				
Assessing Center Time	6				
Flexible Grouping Strategies	6				
Making Grouping Decisions	6				
Assessing the Grouping Scenarios	6				
A/B Partner Sharing	6				
Assessing Partner Teams	6				
Group Assessment Checklist	6				
Group Assessment Scale	6				

Tools and Strategies	Chapter	Before	During	After	Planning Notes
Group Discussion Assessment	6				
Evaluating Group Work	6				
Scoring Individuals in Group Discussions	6				
Self-Assessment for a Group Member	6				
Individual Members Scoring the Group	6				
Assessment of Group Work by an Individual Member	6				
Self-Assessment for a Group Member	6				
Guidelines for Grouping Decisions	6				
Troubleshooting Tools for Group Assessments	6				
Making Appropriate Accommodations During Standardized Tests	7				
Tips for Self-Regulated Test Success	7				
Strategies for the Stumped and Stalled Learner During Tests	7				
Breakthrough Clues for Test Items	7				
Be a Spy for Words That Qualify	7				
Note the Negatives	7				
Thinking Terms	7				
Check, Check, Check	7				
Guidelines to Planning a Parent Conference	7				

Strong preassessments reveal the following qualities of individual students:

- Knowledge base and background experience
- Interests and talents
- Attitudes, likes, and dislikes
- Feelings and emotions

Effective preassessment tools eliminate wasted time and energy in planning. They provide data that circumvents information that is boring or frustrating. It is a challenging and rewarding task to make each lesson meaningful for each learner.

PREASSESSMENT: THE KEY TO ADJUSTABLE ASSIGNMENTS

In the study of a topic, standards are the focus of instruction. Each student has a different knowledge level related to the standard. A great challenge for the teacher is to customize instruction for the various entry levels of the students. The adjustable assignment model identifies students' levels of readiness for the standard, topic, or skill. This allows the teacher to plan instruction within the range of students' abilities, interests, and knowledge levels. The plan is designed to address a range of criteria, varying levels of difficulty, and quantities of information. The adjustable assignment model identifies individual student needs.

The original tiered model was designed by Carol Ann Tomlinson (1999) as a preassessment tool (see Figure 8.4). Following their analysis of the tiered model, Gregory and Chapman (2001, pp. 58–63) designed the adjustable assignment model. Their model adds a step to the tiered model to analyze students' learning levels (see Figure 8.5). At this step, the teacher records the student's specific learning needs. Pinpointing specific needs helps the teacher identify areas where the student needs to "zap the gaps" in the learning, or target instruction to fill in the background information the student or group missed. This is a critical component of instructional planning.

First, analyze what the group on each level knows. Make a specific list. Design or select the preassessment activity that will reveal the student's knowledge level, interests, background, and attitude. Take time to discover the essential pieces. Find the best ways for students to overcome these learning hurdles. Prepare students for the next steps in learning.

In Step III, the authors, Chapman and King (2003b), have added the "how-to" section to each level (see Figure 8.5). Before completing this section, assess the learner, the plan, and the instruction. Use the results to plot

(Text continues on page 198)

Figure 8.4 Degrees of Mastery. Step I: Tiered Model

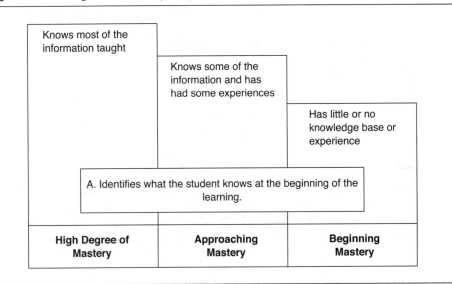

Figure 8.5 Step II: Identify the Learner's Needs

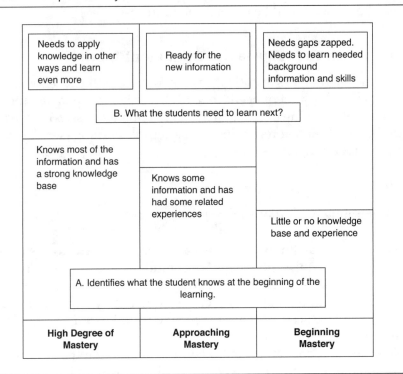

Figure 8.6 Step III: How to Assess

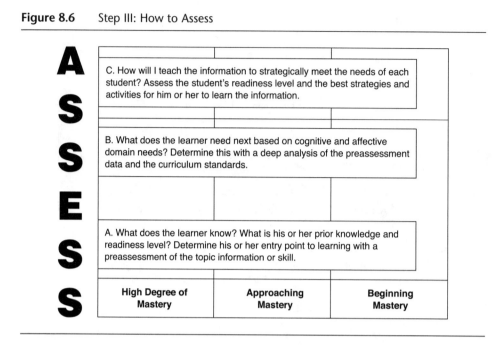

the how-to section as you see the assessment questions cross all mastery levels of the differentiated learners. These assessments are necessary steps because the answers will be different in each case.

Planning With the Adjustable Assignment Model

The teacher analyzes a student's work to identify the level of assistance and instruction the student needs to reach his or her personal learning goals and standards. To guide instruction in a differentiated classroom, the teacher assesses the student before, during, and after the learning (see Figure 8.7).

Try the following steps:

1. Analyze what is happening.

2. Determine what the student knows.

The student may know the information or know how to use a particular skill but keep this knowledge well hidden. The learner may not be aware of what he or she knows about the topic. There may be a lack of focus or concentration. For example, the student may not recognize a new term as it is introduced or may not be able to link prior knowledge with the new learning situation.

When the student cannot tell or write about a new term or topic, the student may be able to show what he or she knows by using a preferred modality, style, intelligence, or genre. This calls for an alternative assessment

Figure 8.7 Adjustable Assignment Model

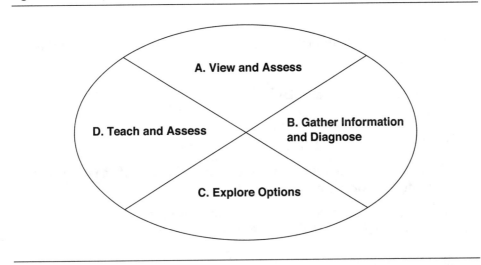

such as showing it, acting it, drawing it, or using it in a real-life situation. Use a personalized assessment tool to give the student more than one opportunity to respond. This is not a waste of time because valuable information is gathered when assessment tools are customized for the learner.

3. Note the student's reaction and behaviors during learning. Examine causes for the actions or lack of response. Why is the student showing excitement or reluctance during the learning?

4. Pinpoint the learner's strengths and weaknesses.

5. Identify the next steps by asking, what does this student need to zap the gaps?

6. Use various instructional and assessment strategies and activities to meet the student's needs.

The Role of Assessment in Curriculum Planning

Assessment plays a major role in curriculum planning. Assessment data informs and guides long- and short-term planning. Various assessment sources provide evidence for curriculum decisions. For example, a teacher may review a student's product, a test, a conference session, and a portfolio to determine future plans.

Analysis of assessment results highlights students' strengths and needs, so the teacher knows how much students can attempt, what they can do, how much they know, and their levels of understanding. The teacher uses this valuable information to identify the next steps for students.

Looking at the Student

A. View and Assess

Describe the student. Include the student's attitudes, interests, preferred ways to learn, strengths, and weaknesses.

B. Gather Information and Diagnose

Explore the information collected.

What does this work tell about how the student learns best?

What are the learner's characteristics or behaviors that will influence his or her performance?

What factors outside the classroom might impact the student's performance?

C. Explore Options. Select Strategies and Activities

Based on what I know about the influences on past performance, which strategies and activities should I plan to better meet the needs of this student?

D. Teach and Assess

How can I make certain that these factors are addressed more thoroughly next time?

Looking at Learning Goals, Objectives, and Expectations

A. View and Assess

Identify the objectives, goals, and standards.

What were you expecting to see in the work?

B. Gather Information and Diagnose

What were the skills, standards, and knowledge learned?

C. Explore Options. Select Strategies and Activities

Does this piece of work show evidence of the objectives being met?

D. Teach and Assess

Identify the information or skills that need reteaching, more practice, and more explanation.

Looking at the Work Sample

A. Observe and Gather Data

What does the work tell me?

What does the student understand or not understand?

B. Analyze the Information and Diagnose

What can I learn from the data to help the student's learning growth?

What are the student's accomplishments toward the learning goals?

What does the student understand? What can the student do?

C. Explore Options. Select Strategies and Activities

What parts still need work?

What needs more explanation?

What gaps remain in the understanding?

D. Teach and Assess

Was instruction productive?

What did the student learn?

What does the student need to learn next?

Looking at the Learner's Prior Experiences and Background Knowledge

A. Observe and Gather Data

What background knowledge or prior experience is evident from examining the student's work?

B. Gather Information and Diagnose

What experiences are lacking that interfere with this student's learning?

What prior knowledge does this student need to enhance his or her learning progress?

C. Explore Options. Select Strategies and Activities

Are these student's prior experiences or background knowledge hindering or promoting learning?

How can I fill in these gaps?

D. Teach and Assess

How are the prior experiences or background knowledge affecting the student's learning now?

What experiences can I add to this part of the teaching?

What is this student's knowledge base?

What does the student need to learn next?

Looking at the Teacher

A. View and Assess

What does this piece of work reveal about the teaching approach?

Were the student's intelligences and learning styles considered?

Were clear directions provided?

Were appropriate materials available?

B. Gather Information and Diagnose

Why was this assignment chosen for this particular student?

What other questions do I have as I look at this work?

Is the mastery of objectives reflected in this work?

Were the objectives accomplished?

C. Explore Options. Select Strategies and Activities

Which strategies and activities worked, and which did not work?

Which strategies and activities have I tried before?

What worked? What did not work?

D. Teach and Assess

What is my plan?

What do I need to do next?

What additional information do I need before I take action?

How will I acquire the information?

SOURCE: *Adapted from the Journal for Staff Development:* Fall 2000 National Staff Development Council. p. 48

ESSENTIAL QUESTIONS FOR PLANNING

Effective teachers cannot be satisfied with a minimum competency or level of mastery learning. The "sit, get, spit, and forget" approach to learning, in which students sit at their desks, get the information, spit it back out on the test, and then forget it, does not benefit students. Teachers may say, "I taught this information!" but the essential question is, did the students learn the information and transfer it to long-term memory for immediate application? Asking ourselves this and related questions can help us stay on track.

> *The central function of assessment, therefore, is not to prove whether or not teaching or learning have taken place, but to improve the quality of teaching and learning, and to increase the likelihood that all members of society will acquire a full and critical literacy.*
>
> —NCTE/IRA Standards for the Assessment of Reading and Writing

Essential Questions

For Teachers and Students

What is the standard, concept, essential question, or benchmark?

What is the purpose or objective?

For Teachers

What do I expect my students to know?

If the student knows the information, how will I know?

How am I going to preassess the knowledge?

How am I going to document, or record, my findings?

What directions do I need to give?

For Students

What do I know?

What am I suppose to know?

How can I show what I know?

What are the directions?

Do I understand each step of the task?

What do I want to learn about this?

What am I looking for?

Which parts are going to be the most interesting for me?

Which parts of the study do I dread?

What questions do I have?

Assess the Assessment Tool

Did this assessment instrument provide a positive experience for students?

Were the students actively engaged in the tasks?

Did the questions uncover the students' knowledge base, prior experiences, and abilities?

Did students understand the directions?

Are there items that need clarification?

Were the assessment tasks within each student's range of success?

Assessment and Technology

Teachers can create an atmosphere where technology enhances learning and assessment processes. Computers are available in most classrooms and can be used to create tests, develop surveys, and design essay prompts, checklists, rubrics, and Likert scales. Special programs make it easy for teachers to record individual student and group data. Assessment results may be shared on the Web, through e-mail, or posted on Web sites. Students' best work can be incorporated in video clip work samples.

Technology enhances learning for students of all abilities in a differentiated classroom in the following ways:

- Assists with instruction and learning
- Assists students of all abilities to learn to use technology in meaningful ways
- Creates opportunities for interaction with others outside the classroom
- Implements instruction on the use of technology
- Provides opportunities to practice, grow, and expand skills
- Enriches learning through discovery
- Facilitates peer learning and reinforces technology learning
- Uses student-based strategies, such as peer tutoring, to enhance and reinforce technology learning
- Offers a range of technology options to meet diverse abilities

EFFECTIVE DIFFERENTIATED ASSESSMENT PRACTICES

As you move forward in differentiating or coaching others, keep in mind the following summary to guide the use of differentiated assessment tools to identify the learner's needs and strengths for strategic planning.

The Chapman and King Differentiating Dozen

1. Use a variety of preassessment tools to identify the learner's knowledge base and prior experiences.

2. Design specific plans to meet the learner's needs.

3. Plan! Plan! Plan!

4. Involve the learner in instructional activities that actively engage him or her in intriguing strategies that help him or her process information for long-term memory.

5. Provide activities that permit students to interact with various assessment tools.

6. Use flexible grouping strategies to optimize learning.

7. Use a variety of assessment tools in multiple formats.

   Conduct surveys through checklists, journal activities, or informal conversations.

8. Plan assessment activities to produce successful experiences for the learner.

9. Teach the learner how to create and apply assessment strategies as a self-directed learner.

10. Provide immediate feedback and assistance, if possible.

11. Emphasize individual growth.

12. Celebrate success.

Evaluating Your Differentiated Assessment Program

When a school embraces differentiated assessment, the quality of the program should be reviewed. Use the following list to evaluate the differentiated assessment program. The criteria are adapted from assessment program standards presented by Stiggins, Webb, Lange, McGregor, and Cotton (1997).

Clear, appropriate expectations are identified.

Practical Applications

- List the required standards, skills, or benchmarks
- Define the expected level of success or mastery for each required item

The assessment serves instructional purposes.

Practical Applications

- Identify who will use the results
- Determine how the results will be used
- Clarify how the data or results improve instruction

Each assessment activity reflects the intended target and provides feedback to all stakeholders.

Practical Applications

- Match assessment tools and activities to individual learners
- Select the feedback formats for the students and parents
- Identify the role of the data in planning differentiated instruction

Sufficient information is provided to generate conclusions related to assessment.

Practical Applications

- Identify instructional objectives based on results
- Share the summary with the learner

Sources are eliminated that may interfere with accuracy of results.

Practical Applications

- Analyze each assessment tool and activity for racial, ethnic, and gender bias
- Remove possible interference and distracting factors
- Consider learners' social and emotional state when interpreting results

Generate change for differentiated assessment approaches through the following:

1. Collaboration: Work together! Each team member must believe differentiated assessment is valuable. Everyone must know that he or she has a vital role as a member of the team.

2. Generating trust and mutual respect! This is earned.

3. Sharing responsibility and creating personal ownership by gathering input from everyone. When everyone participates, every aspect of the teamwork becomes "ours."

4. Assigning each individual team member a role and duties he or she understands and values.

5. Establishing mutual goals: Set priorities and missions to be carried out by the team.

6. Sharing resources: Team members contribute and share resources such as time, talents, space, materials, and equipment.

7. Communicating.

8. Demonstrating interdependence: Members are free to openly contribute their ideas and thoughts to the team.

9. Using differentiated assessment as an ongoing process.

10. Applying evaluation strategies to identify how well goals are accomplished.

11. Sharing accountability in the outcome: Jointly share the results of decisions, both positive and negative.

Supporting Change

Differentiating teachers become models in their larger learning communities. You can support broader change across your school and district in the following ways:

- Create learning communities based on the diverse skills, abilities, and interests of individual students.
- Align goals with those of the school and district.
- Provide continuous leadership for improvement in differentiated instruction and assessment.
- Supply resources and materials.
- Support learning with collaboration that focuses on the uniqueness of each student.

In Conclusion

It is the hope of the authors that the models, strategies, and tools in this book will assist and support the dedicated teachers who make the effort every day to empower all learners as metacognitive, self-directed learners.

References

Airasian, P. W. (2001). *Classroom assessment* (4th ed.). New York: McGraw-Hill.

Arter, J. A., & McTighe, J. (2001). *Scoring rubrics in the classroom.* Thousand Oaks, CA: Corwin Press.

Bandura, A. (1997). *Self efficacy: The exercise of control.* New York: Freeman.

Blachowicz, C., & Fisher, P. (2002). *Teaching vocabulary in all classrooms* (2nd ed.). Columbus, OH: Merrill Prentice-Hall.

Bloom, B. S., & Krathwohl, D. R. (1956). *Taxonomy of educational objectives: The classification of educational goals. Handbook I: Cognitive domain.* New York: Longman, Green.

Bloomfield, D. C., & Cooper, B. S. (2003). No Child Left Behind: A new role for the federal government; an overview of the most sweeping federal education law since 1965. *Technological Horizons in Education Journal, 30*(10).

Bransford, J. D., Brown, A. L., & Cocking, R. R. (Eds.). (1999). *How people learn: Brain, mind, experience, and school.* Washington, DC: National Academic Press.

Brookhart, S. M. (2002). What will teachers know about assessment and how will that improve instruction? In R. W. Kissitz & W. D. Shafer (Eds.), *Assessment in educational reform: Both means and ends.* Needham Heights, MA: Allyn & Bacon.

Burke, K. (1994). *The mindful school: How to assess authentic learning.* Arlington Heights, IL: IRI/SkyLight Training and Publishing.

Caine, R. N., & Caine, G. (1994). *Making connections: Teaching and the human brain.* Menlo Park, CA: Addison-Wesley.

Campbell, D. (2000). Authentic assessment and authentic standards. *Phi Delta Kappan, 81*(5), 404–407.

Carbo, M. (1986). *Teaching students to read in their individual learning styles.* Reston, VA: Prentice-Hall.

Chapman, C. (1993). *If the shoe fits: How to develop multiple intelligences in the classroom.* Arlington Heights, IL: SkyLight.

Chapman, C. & Freeman, L. (1996). *Multiple intelligences through centers and projects.* Arlington Heights, IL: SkyLight.

Chapman, C., & King, R. (2000). *Test success in the brain-compatible classroom.* Tucson, AZ: Zephyr Press.

Chapman, C., & King, R. (2003a). *Differentiated instructional strategies for reading in the content area.* Thousand Oaks, CA: Corwin Press.

Chapman, C., & King, R. (2003b). *Differentiated instructional strategies for writing in the content area.* Thousand Oaks, CA: Corwin Press.

Costa, A. (1991). *The school as a home for the mind.* Palatine, IL: SkyLight.

Costa, P. T., & McRae, R. R. (1998). Personality assessment. In H. S. Friedman (Ed.), *Encyclopedia of mental health* (Vol. 3). San Diego, CA: Academic Press.

Davey, B. (1983). Think aloud: Modeling the cognitive processes of reading comprehension. *Journal of Reading, 27,* 44–47.

DeBono, E. (1985). *Six thinking hats.* Boston: Little, Brown, and Co.

Deci, E. L., Vallerand, R. J., Pelletier, L. G., & Ryans, R. M. (1991). Motivation and education: The self-determination perspective. *Educational Psychologist, 26,* 325–346.

Dempster, F., & Corkill, A. (1999). Interference and inhibition in cognition and behavior: Unifying themes for educational psychology. *Educational Psychology Review, 11*(1), 1–74.

DuFour, R., & Eaker, R. (1998). *Professional learning communities at work: Best practices for enhancing student achievement.* Alexandria, VA: Association for Supervision and Curriculum Development.

Eden, G. F., VanMeter, J. W., Rumsey, J. M., Maisog, J. M., Wood, R. P., & Zeffiro, T. A. (1996). Abnormal processing of visual motion in dyslexia revealed by functional brain imaging. *Nature, 382,* 66–69.

Feist, J., & Feist, G. J. (2002). *Theories of personality* (5th ed.). New York: McGraw-Hill.

Fountas, I., & Pinnell, G. S. (2002). *Guided readers and writers Grades 3–6: Teaching comprehension, genre, and content literacy.* Portsmouth, NH: Heineman.

Gamoran, A., Anderson, C. W., Quiroz, P. A., Secada, W. G., Williams, T., & Ashmann, S. (2003). *Transforming teaching in math and science: How schools and districts can support change.* New York: Teachers College Press.

Garner, H. (1999). *Intelligence reframes: Multiple intelligences for the 21st century.* New York: Basic Books.

Goleman, D. (1995). *Emotional intelligence.* New York: Bantam Books.

Goleman, D. (1998). *Working with emotional intelligence.* New York: Bantam Books.

Gregorc, A. F. (1979). Learning/teaching styles: Potent forces behind them. *Educational Leadership, 36,* 234–237.

Gregorc, A. F. (1982). *Gregorc style delineator—research edition.* Columbia, CT: Gregorc Associates.

Gregory, G. H., & Chapman, C. (2001). *Differentiated instructional strategies: One size doesn't fit all.* Thousand Oaks, CA: Corwin Press.

Hattie, J. (1996). *Self-concept.* Hillsdale, NJ: Erlbaum.

Holloway, J. H. (2000). Preparing teachers for differentiated instruction. *Educational Leadership, 58,* 1.

Hunt, R. R., & Kelley, R. E. S. (1996). Accessing the particular from the general: The power of distinctiveness in the context of organization. *Memory and Cognition, 24,* 210–225.

Hyerle, D. (1990). *Designs for thinking connectively.* Cary, NC: Innovative Systems.

Jensen, E. (1995). *Brain-based learning and teaching.* Del Mar, CA: Turning Point Publishing.

Kolb, D. A. (1984). *Experimental learning.* Englewood Cliffs, NJ: Prentice Hall.

Kolb, D. A. (1985). *Learning style inventory.* Boston, MA: McBer & Co.

Kounin, J. S. (1970). *Discipline and management in classrooms.* New York: Holt, Rinehart, and Winston.

Kusimo, P., Ritter, M., Busick, K., Ferguson, C., Trumbull, E., & Solano-Flores, G. (2000). *Making assessment work for everyone: How to build on student strengths.* Austin, TX: Southwest Educational Development Laboratory.

Lazear, D. (1999). *Multiple intelligence approaches to assessment.* Tucson, AZ: Zephyr Press.

Levine, M. (2002). *One mind at a time.* New York: Simon & Schuster.

Marzano, R. J. (2000). *Transforming classroom grading.* Alexandria, VA: Association for Supervision and Curriculum Development.

Marzano, R. J., Pickering, D. J., & Pollock, J. E. (2001). *Classroom instruction that works: Research-based strategies for increasing student achievement.* Alexandria, VA: Association for Supervision and Curriculum Development.

Merriam-Webster's collegiate dictionary (11th ed.). (2003). Springfield, MA: Merriam-Webster.

Mithaug, D. E., Mithaug, D. K., Martin, A., Martin, J. E., & Wehmeyer, M. (2003). *Self-determined learning memory.* Mahwah, NJ: Lawrence Erlbaum Associates.

Ogle, D. (1986). K-W-L: A teaching model that develops active reading of expository text. *The Reading Teacher, 39,* 564–570.

Otten, L. J., Henson, R. N., & Rugg, M. D. (2001). Depth of processing effects on neural correlates of memory encoding. *Brain, 124,* 399–412.

Pellegrino, J. W (2001). *Knowing what students know: The science and design of educational assessment.* Washington, DC: National Academies Press.

Pettig, K. L. (2000). On the road to differentiated practice. *Educational Leadership, 58*(1), 14–18.

Popham, J. W. (1999). *Classroom assessment: What teachers need to know* (2nd ed.). Boston: Allyn & Bacon.

Reis, S. M., & Purcell, J. H. (1993). An analysis of context elimination and strategies used by elementary classroom teachers in the curriculum compacting process. *Journal for the Education of the Gifted, 16,* 147–170.

Routman, R. (2002). *Conversations: Strategies for teaching, learning, and evaluating.* Portsmouth, NH: Heinemann.

Schunk, D. H. (2000). *Learning theories: An educational perspective* (3rd ed.). Upper Saddle River, NJ: Prentice Hall.

Seuss, Dr. (1996). *My many colored days.* New York: Knopf.

Shepard, L. A. (2000). The role of assessment in a learning culture. *Education Researcher, 29*(7), 4–14.

Silver, H. F., Strong, R. W., & Perini, M. J. (2000). *So each may learn: Integrating learning styles and multiple intelligences.* Alexandria, VA: ASCD.

Sizer, T. R. (2001). No two are quite alike: Personalized learning. *Educational Leadership, 57,* 1.

Sousa, D. (2001). *How the brain learns* (2nd ed.). Thousand Oaks, CA: Corwin Press.

Sprenger, M. (1999). *Learning and memory: The brain in action.* Alexandria, VA: Association for Supervision and Curriculum Development.

Sprenger, M. (2002). *Becoming a "wiz" at brain-based teaching.* Thousand Oaks, CA: Corwin Press.

Stahl, S. A., & Hayes, D. A. (Eds.). (1997). *Instructional models in reading.* Hillsdale, NJ: Lawrence Erlbaum Associates.

Stepanek, M. (2002). *Heartsongs.* New York: Hyperion Press.

Sternberg, R. J. (1997). *Thinking styles.* New York: Cambridge University Press.

Stiggins, R., Webb, L. D., Lange, J., McGregor, S., & Cotton, S. (1997). *Multiple assessment of student progress.* Reston, VA: National Association of Secondary Principals.

Stiggins, R. J. (2001). *Student-involved classroom assessment* (3rd ed.). Upper Saddle River, NJ: Prentice Hall.

Sylwester, R. (2000). Unconscious emotions, conscious feelings. *Educational Leadership, 58*(3), 20–24.

Tierney, R. J., Readence, J. E., & Dishner, E. K. (1995). *Reading strategies and practices: A compendium* (4th ed.). Boston, MA: Allyn & Bacon.

Tomlinson, C. A. (1999). *The differentiated classroom: Responding to the needs of all learners.* Alexandria, VA: Association for Supervision and Curriculum Development

Vygotsky, L. S. (1978). *Mind in society.* M. Cole, V. John-Steiner, S. Scribner, & E. Souberman (Eds.). Cambridge, MA: Harvard University Press.

Webster's new world college dictionary (4th ed.). (2001). Foster City, CA: IDG Books Worldwide.

Wiggins, G. (1993). *Assessing student performance.* San Francisco: Jossey-Bass.

Willis, S., & Mann, L. (2000, Winter). *Differentiating instruction: Finding manageable ways to meet individual needs.* Retrieved August 1, 2004, from http://www.ascd.org/cms/objectlib/ascdframeset/index.cfm?publication=http://www.ascd.org/publications/curr_update/2000winter/willis.html

Wormeli, R. (2001). Aim for more authentic assessment. *Middle Ground: The Magazine of Middle Level Education, 4,* 3.

Index